Contents

CW01523124

YORK NOTES

General Editors: Professor A.N. Jeffares (*University of Stirling*) & Professor Suheil Bushrui (*American University of Beirut*)

T. S. Eliot

FOUR QUARTETS

Notes by Maire A. Quinn

MA PH D (QUEEN'S UNIVERSITY, BELFAST)
Lecturer in English, Trinity College, Dublin

LONGMAN
YORK PRESS

YORK PRESS
Immeuble Esseily, Place Riad Solh, Beirut.

LONGMAN GROUP LIMITED
Burnt Mill,
Harlow, Essex

© Librairie du Liban 1982

First published 1982
ISBN 0 582 78252 X

Printed in Hong Kong by
Sing Cheong Printing Co Ltd

Part 1

Introduction

Life of T.S. Eliot

Thomas Stearns Eliot was born into a prosperous and cultivated family in St Louis, Missouri, on 26 September 1888. This town was to provide the setting for 'The Love Song of J. Alfred Prufrock', while in 'The Dry Salvages' Eliot recalls his early memories of the Mississippi river. His father's family had emigrated to the United States from the English village of East Coker, Somerset, in the seventeenth century, and this ancestral village features in the second of *Four Quartets*. In 1906 Eliot went to Harvard where he read classics, modern languages and ancient history. He went to Paris for a year to study French literature and philosophy at the Sorbonne in 1910 and returned to Harvard the following year to read for a Ph.D. His thesis on the philosophy of F.H. Bradley was completed in 1916 but was not published until 1964, when it appeared under the title *Knowledge and Experience in the Philosophy of F.H. Bradley*.

In 1914 Eliot left Harvard for England and spent his last year as a student of philosophy at Oxford. England was to be his home for the rest of his life. He became a British citizen in 1927. While at Harvard Eliot had written 'The Love Song of J. Alfred Prufrock' and in England he immediately began an acquaintance with Ezra Pound (1895–1972) who recognised his genius and promoted his poetry. In June 1915 Eliot married Vivien Haigh-Wood, a marriage which was to cause him much unhappiness. He was now forced to earn a living and became a schoolmaster for a couple of years. In 1917 he joined Lloyds Bank in London where he remained for eight years during which he wrote some of his finest poetry. His first collection of poems, *Prufrock and Other Observations*, was published in June 1917 and his second, *Poems*, also known as *Ara Vos Prec*, in 1920. He found a small but distinguished audience on both sides of the Atlantic. Eliot also worked on two influential literary magazines, acting as literary editor of *The Egoist* between 1917 and 1919 and as editor of *The Criterion* from 1922 to 1939. This involved an immense amount of literary criticism. His two early collections of critical essays, *The Sacred Wood* (1920) and *Homage to John Dryden* (1924), between them effected a revolution in critical taste.

Eliot's thoughts had turned to the composition of a long poem and he was at work on *The Waste Land* by 1921. In October of that year his health broke down and he was given leave of absence from Lloyds. While convalescing at Margate and in Lausanne, Switzerland, he completed *The Waste Land*, which was published in 1922. It met with a mixed reception from established critics but was greeted enthusiastically by the younger generation. 'The Hollow Men' appeared in 1925 and in that year, too, Eliot left the bank and joined the newly formed publishing house of Faber and Gwyer where he worked for the remainder of his life. In 1927 he was converted to Christianity and the spiritual trauma of his conversion is reflected in his poems 'Journey of the Magi' (1927) and 'A Song for Simeon' (1928). He went on to write religious poetry of great beauty and authority in *Ash Wednesday* (1927–30) and *Four Quartets* (1936–42). After 1942 he wrote no significant poetry.

For several years Eliot had been interested in drama and had discussed his ideas on the subject in essays and reviews. His first attempt at writing for the stage was the unfinished pageant play *The Rock*. *Sweeney Agonistes* was produced in 1934 and *Murder in the Cathedral*, which deals with the martyrdom of Thomas à Becket, followed in 1935. Eliot moved into his contemporary world with *The Family Reunion* (1939), *The Cocktail Party* (1949), *The Confidential Clerk* (1954) and *The Elder Statesman* (1958). These verse dramas of the 1950s mark the final phase of Eliot's career as a creative writer.

By the late 1940s Eliot was a public figure, widely renowned as a major poet and critic. In 1948 he was awarded the Nobel Prize for Literature. In that year, too, his wife, from whom he had been long separated, died, and in 1957 he married his secretary, Valerie Fletcher. The last years of Eliot's life were happy ones. Despite ill-health he continued to travel and to lecture. He died in 1965 aged seventy-six.

Intellectual background

From 1928 onwards Eliot was concerned increasingly with the manner in which social and political factors impinge upon the work of the artist. He was conscious of the fact that the poet exists in a specific historical situation but because of his conversion to Christianity his philosophy of life was at odds with contemporary trends and beliefs in Western society. Three of the quartets were written during the Second World War and the historic situation in which Eliot found himself made a decided impact on his poetry. However, his diagnosis of the plight of civilisation and the remedies he proposes are expressed in uncompromisingly Christian terms. Whereas *The Waste Land* reflects a representative modern sensibility, *Four Quartets* is a dogmatic poem whose teachings are not representative of the age in which it was written. *Four Quartets* does not regard man as the influential psychologist Sigmund Freud (1856–1939) represented him. For Freud man is a biological phenomenon. He is simply a part of nature, a prey to his instincts which he redirects as far as is necessary to accommodate himself to reality. Eliot would have found himself in disagreement also with the views of Karl Marx (1818–83) which enjoyed a vogue in English intellectual circles in the 1930s. Marxists considered man to be the outcome of economic and social forces, the product of an evolution in society comparable to the evolution in nature observed by Charles Darwin (1809–82). Again Eliot's ideas were at variance with the scientific humanist standpoint as represented by Bertrand Russell (1872–1970), one of England's leading philosophers, who held that man's aspirations and hopes were 'but the outcome of chance collocations of atoms'. Man, for Eliot, belongs both to a natural and to a supernatural world. He is inherently the child of sin and owes his possibility of salvation to the grace of God. He is a free, self-determining being, who uses his freedom wrongly when he sins. Since the post-1927 Eliot is a committed Anglican who is strongly opposed to all other interpretations of human life, an understanding of contemporary trends in psychology, economics, sociology and philosophy will not help to illuminate *Four Quartets* for us. Instead it may be helpful to ponder the relationship between Eliot's pre-Christian and post-Christian phase in order to understand the significance of Christianity for his art.

At Harvard Eliot was deeply influenced by two of his professors, the philosopher George Santayana (1863–1952) and the critic and cultural historian Irving Babbitt (1865–1933). Both stressed the relationship of literary and social values. Although he later disagreed with Babbitt's humanism, Eliot owed to this early teacher his lifelong dislike of Romanticism and allegiance to Classicism. The ideals of Classicism for Eliot were form and restraint in art, discipline and authority in religion, centralisation in government and austerity in the business of living. Babbitt taught that even if modern man does not submit to some definite doctrine or philosophy as his ancestors did, nevertheless, he must acknowledge some higher authority. Eliot's entire career was built upon the search for this higher authority. When his interests were primarily literary he looked for it in tradition; as his interests turned towards religion he found it in Christian dogma.

'Tradition and the Individual Talent' is the central essay in Eliot's early collection of critical essays *The Sacred Wood* (1920). Here his impatience with Romanticism, his sense of the insufficiency of the individual, is manifest. The essay records Eliot's certainty that any truly significant modern work must be built upon the achievements of the past. 'No poet, no artist of any art has his complete meaning alone,' he writes. The essay on the English Romantic poet William Blake (1757–1827) in *The Sacred Wood* affords Eliot an opportunity to display the weakness of Romanticism while the essay on the medieval Italian poet

Dante (1265–1321) is used as a demonstration of the strengths of Classicism. The reason for Dante's being regarded as a classic and Blake only a poet of genius is that Dante had a coherent system of theology, philosophy and metaphysics on which to draw and was therefore able to devote his entire energies to the writing of poetry, whereas Blake had to forge his own system. Lacking such a coherent framework of belief himself, in *The Waste Land* Eliot drew heavily on mythology and literature to give shape and significance to 'the intense panorama of futility and anarchy' that was contemporary history. *The Waste Land* is a monument to Eliot's belief in the importance to the artist of a literary tradition.

By 1928, however, Eliot had found an authoritative philosophical and moral framework in the beliefs of the Church of England, and his new position is outlined in a collection of essays entitled *For Lancelot Andrewes*. Eliot's decision to join the Church was a process that occurred 'perhaps insensibly, over a long period of time'. It does not admit of simple explanation and in *For Lancelot Andrewes* he does not seek to explain it. Most of the essays testify to his increased interest in moral and religious issues. In discussing such writers as Machiavelli (1469–1527), Middleton (1570?–1627), Crashaw (1612?–49) and Baudelaire (1821–67) he comments on the religious significance of their work. He also points out the inadequacy of the humanist position in an essay on his former teacher, Irving Babbitt. The preface to *For Lancelot Andrewes* contains the famous announcement that Eliot's point of view is now 'classicist in literature, royalist in politics, and anglo-catholic in religion'. The meeting-place of these three positions lay in early seventeenth-century England. As early as 1921 Eliot had been an admirer of the Metaphysical poets but now his regard for the period extended to include the 'intellectual achievement and prose style' of the English theologians Richard Hooker (1554?–1600) and Bishop Lancelot Andrewes (1555–1626) and the spiritual leadership of Archbishop Laud (1573–1645). In 'Little Gidding' Eliot makes an imaginative pilgrimage to seventeenth-century England. Little Gidding is a shrine to Royalist and Anglo-Catholic values since its founder, Nicholas Ferrar (1592–1637), was a follower of Laud, defender of the Anglican Church, who gave refuge to King Charles I.

Earlier in *Four Quartets* Eliot had also paid tribute to another and contrary intellectual influence, that of Oriental philosophy and religion which he had studied in the graduate school at Harvard. In *The Waste Land* he brought together Buddha and the Roman Catholic theologian St Augustine (345–430) as representives of Eastern and Western asceticism and found the resolution of the poem's conflict in the words of the thunder from the *Upanishads*, which form part of the Hindu sacred writings. In *Four Quartets* he drew on the *Bhagavadgita*, also part of the Hindu scriptures. Although he spoke of his difficulty in understanding Indian philosophy in *After Strange Gods* (1933), he acknowledged in 1948 that his poetry shows 'the influence of Indian thought and sensibility'.

Literary background

There was no current tradition in English poetry on which Eliot felt that he could draw, so from the beginning we find him basing his style on foreign, or unfamiliar English models. His enthusiasm for the English Romantics was an affair of adolescence and by 1908 he had discovered Arthur Symons's (1865–1945) *The Symbolist Movement in Literature* (1899), which introduced him to the French poets Baudelaire (1821–67), Verlaine (1844–96), Rimbaud (1854–91) and Laforgue (1860–87). Symbolist poetry was indirect and allusive, its words and images being arranged in such a way as to set up a complex pattern of associations. It concentrated on evoking moods and states of feeling, usually those of pain, guilt and loneliness. From Laforgue, who treated such themes with self-mocking humour, Eliot learned an ironic, self-deprecating manner of speaking as a way of distancing painful, intimate experience. Laforgue's influence may be discerned in 'The Love Song of J. Alfred Prufrock', completed in 1911. Among English poets Eliot favoured Shakespeare and the then unfashionable Jacobean dramatists and Metaphysical poets. After his move to England in 1914 Eliot was befriended by Ezra Pound, a leader of the Imagist group of poets. Like the Symbolists the Imagists wanted a pure poetry, exclusive of all extra-poetic content, and they encouraged the practice of free verse. The Imagists stressed the need for austerity and discipline in poetry. They rejected infinity, mystery and indulgence in emotions and favoured a dry, hard, sculptured verse. In maintaining that the image is the primary pigment of poetry they, in the words of the English poet, Stephen Spender (b.1909), 'isolated the basic unit of the modern poem'. Both Symbolism and Imagism are early manifestations of what is known as Modernism, the dominant tendency of twentieth-century art.

Modernism in all the arts is characterised by experimentation, by a fascination with technical innovation. Modernist poetry tends to avoid the unity of mood characteristic of Romantic poetry and instead has recourse to juxtapositions, tonal shifts and the presentation of multiple viewpoints. It eschews narrative or chronological ordering of its materials and explores alternative methods of aesthetic ordering such as allusion to or imitation of literary models and mythical archetypes and the repetition-with-variation of motifs. The handling of time is complex, involving much cross-reference backwards and forwards. The reader of a Modernist text is not asked to follow the story but to discern a design and the unity of the work results from its entire pattern of internal references, what is often referred to as its 'spatial form'. Examples of early Modernist works are Joyce's *Ulysses* (1922), Virginia Woolf's *To the Lighthouse* (1927), Lawrence's *Women in Love* (1920), Pound's *Hugh Selwyn Mauberley* (1920) and Yeats's *The Tower* (1928). Eliot's *The Waste Land* is his first major poem in the Imagist/Modernist mode. It also endorses Eliot's belief in the necessity of tradition for the artist since it is a work in which the 'dead poets, his ancestors, assert their immortality most vigorously'. Many of his favourite authors are alluded to or quoted from or parodied. These include the dramatists William Shakespeare (1564–1616), Thomas Middleton (1570?–1627), John Webster (1580?–1625?) and the poets Andrew Marvell (1621–78), Dante and Baudelaire.

Dante's poetry, Eliot said in 1950, was the 'most persistent and deepest influence' on his own verse. Eliot's enthusiasm for this master was not confined to matters of technique and craftsmanship. Dante embodied for Eliot what he called in 'Tradition and the Individual Talent' the 'mind of Europe'. He considered *The Divine Comedy* to be the great central poetic expression of the Christian system, the highest example of poetry based on a consistent philosophy. *The Divine Comedy*, which Dante composed between 1307 and 1321, is a long and complex poem divided into three parts, *Inferno* (Hell), *Purgatorio* (Purgatory) and *Paradiso* (Paradise). The literal subject of the work is the journey that Dante makes through these three regions, but the poem really expresses Dante's religious, moral and political conception of the universe and of man's role in it. Dante dominated Eliot's poetry from the words of Guido da Montefeltro at the beginning of 'Prufrock' to the superb Dantesque recreation in 'Little Gidding'. The particular passages from *The Divine Comedy* which haunted Eliot's imagination were those based on an encounter between the living poet and one of the dead poets, his ancestors. Over and over again he alluded to the Arnaut Daniel passage in *Purgatorio* XXVI, but the most significant of all such confrontations for Eliot was that of Dante and Brunetto Latini in *Inferno* XV. Eliot referred to the episode in the *Sacred Wood* essay on Dante, in 'Tradition and the Individual Talent' and in the 1929 essay on Dante, and it provided the model for the Dantesque scene in 'Little Gidding'.

By the time he came to write *Four Quartets* Eliot was writing as a Christian poet, like his beloved Dante, but he was doing so in a Modernist mode. *Four Quartets* may be less obviously revolutionary because its structure is more orderly than that of *The Waste Land*. However, Eliot is still an exponent of the ideal of 'spatial form' in poetry. The structure of *Four Quartets* is musical rather than chronological or narrative and its unity depends on a complex pattern of internal echoes.

A note on the text

Four Quartets was not originally conceived as a sequence of four poems. The idea of a unified poem composed of four separate poems only suggested itself to Eliot as he was writing the second poem in the series. 'Burnt Norton', the first of the quartets, was composed in the latter part of 1935 in an interval between the completion of *Murder in the Cathedral* and the start of *The Family Reunion*. Eliot tells us that it took shape through a catalysing of various fragments discarded from *Murder in the Cathedral*. He wrote it quickly and it was ready in time to be included as the final poem in his *Collected Poems 1909–1935*, Faber and Faber, London, 1936. Eliot then became absorbed in the problems of writing for the stage and might have gone straight from *The Family Reunion* to another play had not the Second World War intervened. The war destroyed his dramatic interests for a time and made him more introspective. 'East Coker', which followed the pattern of 'Burnt Norton', was the result. It was printed as a supplement to the *New English Weekly* Easter number in 1940 and was so enthusiastically received that the supplement was reprinted three times. In September, the poem was published as a Faber shilling pamphlet. The notion of a cycle of four poems based on the symbolism of the four elements and the four seasons came to Eliot during the writing of 'East Coker'. 'The Dry Salvages' appeared in *New English Weekly* in February 1941 and, like its predecessor, was published as a Faber pamphlet in September. 'Burnt Norton' had already been published in this form in February 1941. 'Little Gidding' proved slower and more difficult to write than the previous three quartets. It was the hardest to write because it had to complete the shape of the sequence and crown the entire achievement. Eliot was afraid that he might simply repeat himself and parody the earlier poems in the group. The Dantesque passage in the second movement proved particularly troublesome. Finally, 'Little Gidding' was completed to Eliot's satisfaction and was printed in *New English Weekly* in October 1942. It was published in pamphlet form in December. *Four Quartets* in its entirety appeared first in America in May 1943. The English edition did not appear until October 1944. In these editions of the poem the Greek epigraphs were printed on the reverse of the table of contents, as if they applied to the sequence as a whole. In the *Collected Poems 1909–1962*, however, they were printed as part of 'Burnt Norton' as had originally been the case.

Four Quartets is also published separately by Faber in paperback, tenth impression 1979.

Part 2

Summaries
of FOUR QUARTETS

A general summary

As the title suggests, the art of *Four Quartets* aspires to music rather
than to narrative and it, therefore, resists the idea of a summary. What
follows is a necessarily crude description of the arrangement of ideas
in each quartet.

Each of the quartets takes its title from the name of a place.

'Burnt Norton', the most abstract of the four quartets, is concerned
with the nature of life in time. Paradoxically, because we live in time we
can overcome the limitations imposed by time which are its division
into past, present and future. We have access even to what might have
been. All existence in the universe is part of a repetitive pattern. One
rarely arrives at a still point from which the whole pattern may be dis-
cerned because such an experience is too intense. The only way of
escape from the trivial round of life is through the mystical way of
purgation. Although life seems to be sequential it conforms to a design
like a work of art. Only the love of God is unmoving. The element of
this quartet is air.

In 'East Coker' Eliot returns to the place of his family origins and
meditates on the relationship between the beginning and end of human
life. He looks back to the rituals of his ancestors and forward to the
pitfalls of old age. He writes during the Second World War (1939–45),
which is a time of darkness and disorientation, but he considers that
such suffering may be good for the soul. The negative way of the mystics
is the proper way to conduct one's life. He follows this by a lyric on the
spiritual plight of fallen man. Finally, he comments on his own con-
tinued experimentation as a poet and concludes that all life must be an
adventure towards union with God. The element of this quartet is
earth.

In 'The Dry Salvages' Eliot returns to his childhood world, focusing
in particular on river and sea imagery. Both river and sea testify to
universal forces beyond human control. The boredom and the horror
of life are portrayed through the metaphor of life at sea. This metaphor
is then expanded to embrace other forms of travel and Eliot admonishes
us to live for today as Krishna, the great deity of later Hinduism, coun-
sels in the *Bhagavadgita*, concentrating on action rather than on results.
He prays to the Virgin Mary on behalf of all voyagers. Finally, he

depicts man's foolish preoccupation with past and future and the more rewarding life of those who experience moments of ecstasy and are content to discipline their lives in preparation for such timeless moments. The element of this quartet is water.

In 'Little Gidding' Eliot visits a shrine which has associations with the religious life of England in time of war. Little Gidding is a holy place which can change men's lives. Eliot dwells on the unleashing of destructive forces in the universe and on the horrors of old age. He cultivates an attitude of detachment based on the mystical revelation that 'all shall be well'. He now sees the Second World War as a divine visitation by which God in his love is purifying man. He concludes that although the progress of life is towards death this is the necessary prelude to a new beginning. His poem then circles back to include images from earlier phases and finishes with an image of redemption achieved through suffering. The element of this quartet is fire.

Detailed summaries

Title

The title Eliot originally had in mind was *Kensington Quartets*. He had lived in Kensington in south-west London from the end of 1933 until November 1940. 'Burnt Norton' and 'East Coker' were both written during this period. Although he wrote the later quartets after he had moved to a village near Guildford their roots lay in the Kensington period. This period had a deep personal significance for Eliot since he regarded it as a time of reconstruction and reorientation after the close of a distressful chapter in his life. (He had obtained a legal separation from his wife in 1933.) However, Eliot was persuaded to drop the word 'Kensington' from the title since, to those who were unaware of its private significance, the place-name would have conjured up a picture of shabby respectability and the keeping up of outmoded conventions. Although Eliot felt that there might be objections to the use of a musical analogy in the title of a poem he decided to refer to the collection as *Four Quartets*. The word 'quartets', he thought, would put readers on the right track for understanding the poems. He wanted to indicate that they were all written in a particular set form which he had elaborated. 'Sonata' was too musical a term for what he had in mind. 'Quartet' suggested to Eliot the notion of making a poem by weaving together three or four superficially unrelated themes so that they form a new whole.

'Burnt Norton'

Title: In the summer of 1934 Eliot, on a vacation in Gloucestershire, visited an uninhabited mansion at Aston Subedge and wandered in its formal garden. This house had been erected on the site of an earlier country house burnt two hundred years before. The experience provided the poem with its title and one of its central images. It has no particular personal associations for Eliot but it suggests a way of life which is social and civilised, cultured and refined.

Epigraphs: Both are fragments from Diel's edition of the writings of the Greek philosopher Heraclitus (*c.*500BC). The first may be translated 'Although the Word (Logos) is common to all, most people live as if each of them had a private intelligence of his own', and the second 'The way up and the way down are one and the same'.

I. 'Burnt Norton' is the most abstract and the most difficult of the four quartets. It opens with a meditation on time in which the word 'time' itself appears seven times in five lines. The speaker comments on the possible relationship of present, past and future and speculates that such temporal divisions may be an illusion and that all time may be eternally present. The poem then focuses on the past, on 'what might have been' more than on what actually has been, and indicates that our personal past is conceivable only because we exist in the present. At this point Eliot begins to use images rather than abstract language. The memory of 'What might have been' is envisaged as a passage leading to an unopened door and an unvisited rose-garden. The first person plural is also introduced for the first time implying that what is being described is a common experience. This is borne out by the fact that before exploring the garden the speaker addresses someone, presumably the reader, suggesting that they have a shared understanding. From now on throughout the movement the first person plural is used, implicating the reader in the happenings of the poem. The reference to 'the dust on a bowl of rose-leaves' is evidence that the rose-garden of the 'might have been' has been visited some time before. The rose-leaves have been gathered long enough to have become dusty. The garden is explored in the following paragraph. It is the formal garden of a stately home with alleys, boxwood hedges and a lotus-pool. The guide is a thrush, the season is autumn and the garden itself, although deserted, is full of insubstantial and unseen presences. At the beginning these are dignified adult presences and later they behave with the courtesy of guests but by the end of the paragraph the hidden people are like giggling children playing hide-and-seek. The bird who had initially invited speaker and reader to visit the garden now orders them to depart, declaring that human beings cannot endure very much reality.

The final lines of the first movement repeat certain phrases about the nature of time from the early part of the movement.

The garden as well as being an image of the 'might have been' is also referred to as 'our first world', signifying both the world of childhood and the biblical Garden of Eden. This is probably the point being made in the sentence 'Other echoes / Inhabit the garden'. The allusion to childhood is picked up at the end of the paragraph where the leaves are 'full of children'. The fact that the garden is deserted conjures up the notion of the Garden of Eden which Adam and Eve were forced to abandon after they had sinned. In Christian terms the Garden of Eden represents 'what might have been' for 'human kind'.

The first half of the movement is speculative and the diction creates an effect of uncertainty through the use of words such as 'perhaps', 'if', 'possibility', 'do not know'. Many of the nouns are abstract. The appeal is to the mind of the reader. The second part of the movement, on the other hand, is colloquial and full of concrete nouns. It is also full of action, unlike the first part which is static. A change of pace is indicated by the word 'quick', and the repetition of 'find them' also conveys urgency. Motion is signified by such words as 'follow', 'round', 'through', 'into', 'moving', 'over' 'along'. When this movement is brought to a halt by the side of the pool the bird's imperative 'Go, go, go' renews the sense of urgency by repeating a verb of movement.

Eliot's philosophical point that the 'has been' and the 'might have been' 'Point to one end which is always present' is reinforced by his choice and placing of grammatical tense in this movement. In the first part all the principal verbs are in the present tense and the past tense is used only in a subordinate capacity. The second part which undertakes an excursion into the 'might have been' is written in the past tense for the most part, as one would expect, but it begins and ends in the present tense. The entire first movement is also framed by sentences written in the present tense and by the word 'present' itself. Its first words are 'Time present' and its last 'always present'. The present is, therefore, in a position of grammatical and structural dominance in the first movement.

NOTES AND GLOSSARY:

containing laughter: this may mean 'full of laughter' or 'restraining laughter'

human kind ... reality: this was said by St Thomas à Becket at the close of his last speech to the Chorus before his martyrdom in *Murder in the Cathedral*

II. The second movement opens with a short rhymed lyric which describes the patterning of the universe. This pattern is repeated at all levels from the lowest to the highest, so the lyric begins with 'mud' and ends 'among the stars'. Its motions are those of ascent and descent. The 'axle-tree' would appear to be Yggdrasil, which is rooted in earth but reaches towards the heavens and, therefore, represents a union of earthly and heavenly phenomena. Eliot focuses first of all on the earthy base of Yggdrasil and then ascends from the vegetable (garlic) and mineral (sapphires) level to the animal and human level with the image of the circulation of the blood. The notion of reconciliation is introduced when life is depicted as making peace with the wars of the past. The motion of ascent is continued as the movements of bodily circulation are compared to the movement of the stars. The axle-tree now reappears but this time the focus is on its leaves which are patterned and catch the light. The correspondence between its foliage and the constellations of stars is emphasised by the use of the word 'figured' to refer to both. Our attention is directed to the worlds 'above' and 'below' the axle-tree. The pattern of pursuit and animal desire on earth is repeated in the heavens but there what was separated is reconciled. Since Eliot's theme is the patterning of the universe he writes in a highly patterned manner. Although the lyric is not broken into verses it is composed of a series of triplets in which one rhyme from each triplet is repeated in the next. The triple pattern is repeated by the use of a line of three stresses.

From the imagistic mode of the lyric Eliot now moves on to a philosophical meditation in abstract language using a much longer poetic line. The notion of the axle of the universe is reintroduced but it is now presented in abstract terms as the 'still point of the turning world'. We are here being confronted with the paradox of the philosopher's wheel, the exact centre of which is motionless, whatever the velocity of the rim. Eliot depicts it as a point at which opposites are cancelled out. However, he wants to show that it is an energising point as well as a point of cancellation, so he resorts to the image of the dance, an image of patterned movement. Eliot now introduces the idea of the timeless moment in human life which is to be one of the key ideas in *Four Quartets*. Its significance will become clearer as the poem proceeds. Here it corresponds to 'the still point of the turning world' except that it has a personal rather than a cosmic relevance. Like the 'still point' it is described in negative terminology in the beginning, defined by what it is not, rather than by what it is. It is a point at which one is freed from normal human constraints, a point of pure consciousness in which we see into the life of things and understand both the ecstasy and horror of the world. Eliot had remarked, in 'Burnt Norton' I, that 'human kind/ Cannot bear very much reality'. Here he makes a similar point about man's inability to endure agony and ecstasy. Usually, one is protected from a full realisation of heaven and hell by transience, the passage of time and the changes to which the human body is subject. The moment of pure consciousness is outside the processes of time but we are dependent on time in order to remember such a moment. We can only remember what is past. Eliot lists a number of moments which one might wish to preserve through memory. The moment in the rose-garden looks back to 'Burnt Norton' I. The moment in the draughty church seems to anticipate 'Little Gidding', but since 'Little Gidding' was not conceived when this poem was written it is more likely to be a private reference to Eliot's reception into the Church of England. The moment in the arbour does not refer to any experience from within the poem.

The second part of the second movement is dogmatic. Eliot speaks in the first person singular but with the voice of an authoritative public lecturer rather than a private man. He makes pronouncements and tells us what to think: 'And do not call it fixity . . .'. However, at least two of the images at the end of the movement have only a private relevance so that we conclude with the impression that the public statements are derived from personal experience.

NOTES AND GLOSSARY:

Garlic and sapphires . . . axle-tree: these lines are based on an adaptation of two phrases taken from the French symbolist poet Mallarmé (1842–98). The first is *'Tonnerre et rubis aux moyeux'* (Thunder and rubies on the axles), from the poem *'M'introduire dans ton histoire'*. The second is *'bavant boue et rubis'* (spluttering out mud and rubies), from the sonnet *'Le Tombeau de Charles Baudelaire'*. The combination of 'garlic' and 'sapphires' suggests the union of such opposites as vegetable and mineral, soft and hard, living and petrified, common and precious, rank-smelling and odourless

axle-tree: the axle of the turning heavens. Like Yggdrasil, the world tree which represents all living nature in Scandinavian mythology, it is embedded in earth. The union of earthly and heavenly phenomena is a theme of the lyric as a whole

trilling wire in the blood: the nervous tingling in our veins. The image is that of the telegraph wire

At the still point of the turning world: Eliot used this phrase in 'Coriolan I: Triumphal March' (1931)

Erhebung: (*German*) the still point

III. 'Burnt Norton' II ended with a series of visionary moments. The third movement begins by focusing on the 'waste, sad time stretching before and after' such moments. The words 'before' and 'after' are repeated like a refrain throughout this paragraph. A state of death-in-life is being conveyed in terms of place. Eliot has discovered a modern image of the underworld in the London Underground. He also exploits lighting effects to suggest a state of half-life. The Underground, or 'tube', has neither the worldly beauty conferred by light nor the spiritual beauty conferred by darkness. This reference to 'the dark night of the soul' will be developed in the next paragraph. The presentation of life as a journey and of people as passengers is a recurrent motif in *Four Quartets*. The tube passengers depicted here are anxious but lack all sense of purpose. The wretchedness of the Underground station is evoked to suggest a state of spiritual wretchedness. The station is swept by cold winds, strewn with scraps of paper, its air is stale and unwholesome. At the end of the paragraph Eliot, continuing with his wind imagery, depicts the whole of London as spiritually polluted by the belching of unhealthy souls. From the Underground the last lines ascend to the seven hills of London and then the next paragraph begins with a motion of descent. This paragraph had begun with the word 'here'. It is dismissed with a repetition of the phrase, 'not here'.

The second paragraph proposes an escape from the boredom and horror of life through asceticism. What Eliot is describing is the negative way advocated by such mystics as St John of the Cross. It involves a life of self denial, solitude, darkness, the foregoing of sensual delights and fanciful distractions. One can descend to God either by strenuous effort (movement) or by remaining passive (abstention from movement). These two means of spiritual descent were suggested to Eliot by the alternative means of descent in the tube station, the stairs and the lift. At the close of the section the 'Time before and time after' of the previous paragraph are changed to 'time past and time future'. The railway also recurs and is presented as an image of that worldly life in time from which the ascetic has escaped. In this paragraph Eliot is attempting the difficult task of writing a poetry of negation. The world is nullified over and over again, first through a repetition of the phrase, 'not world', and then through a series of parallel phrases in which significant areas of human experience are cancelled out, for instance, 'deprivation/And destitution of . . . Desiccation of . . .', and so on. Movement, associated with ordinary life in time, is depicted not as something vital and various but as a boring journey along narrow, predetermined tracks.

NOTES AND GLOSSARY:

disaffection: the word is used in all of its three senses: (*i*) the absence or alienation of affection; (*ii*) alienation from or discontent with existing authority; (*iii*) physical disorder, or diseased condition

darkness to purify the soul: this refers to the mystical experience described by St John of the Cross (1542–91), as 'the dark night of the soul', a purgation of the sense, fancy and spirit which the soul must undergo if it is to be united with God. St John of the Cross, a Carmelite monk, is renowned as a Spanish lyric poet and as one of the great mystics of all time. His fame rests on three poems, 'Dark Night', 'Spiritual Canticle' and 'Living Flame of Love', and on four commentaries upon these poems which bear the same titles except that 'Dark Night' inspired a second commentary entitled *The Ascent of Mount Carmel*. Mysticism in his writings consists of the three stages of purgation, illumination and union with God. Two of his favourite images, those of the 'dark night' and of 'flame' and 'fire', are used by Eliot in *Four Quartets*

Eructation: belching. Eliot is making use of wind imagery in this paragraph

gloomy hills: seven hills are named, a parody of the seven hills of the eternal city, Rome

Internal darkness, deprivation: this and the following four lines refer again to 'the dark night of the soul'. The idea is that the soul cannot be united with the Divine until it has divested itself of the love of created things

appetency: longing or desire. The traditional word to describe this state is 'concupiscence'

metalled ways: railroad tracks. The underlying image in this section is the London Underground railway system

IV. Time and movement are treated imagistically in this brief lyric. Natural images recall the garden setting of the first movement but are here used to convey darkness and death. Sunset is presented in funereal terms through the words 'bell', 'buried' and 'black'. The sunflower and clematis droop earthwards and the phrase 'Clutch and cling' carries the sinister implication of a drowning person's grip. The reference to 'Chill/ Fingers of yew' prolongs the sinister effect and continues the downward movement. It also contributes to the funereal imagery since the yew tree is usually found growing in cemeteries and has connotations of death and burial. Like the sun the kingfisher appears as an image of transient natural light. Despite the onset of darkness the universe is not utterly deprived of light. Light is present 'at the still point of the turning world'. This echoes a line from the second movement, a deliberate reminder that darkness like light is due to the revolving nature of the universe and, therefore, not to be feared. Eliot puns on the word 'still' in the first instance, using it as a grammatical term but also to evoke an atmosphere of tranquillity. The shape of this lyric reflects its negative and positive approach to the theme of transience. Eliot employs a device of diminution and increase in the line lengths and in the number of stressed syllables per line to suggest fear and the restoration of calm. The design is similar to that of the metaphysical poet George Herbert's (1593-1633) 'Easter Wings' but the correspondences in Eliot's lyric are not as precisely worked out as in Herbert's.

V. In this final part of 'Burnt Norton' Eliot extends his meditation on time and movement to the realm of art and, in particular, to words and music, the art of poetry. What exercises Eliot here is the problem of the permanence of sequential arts like literature and music. The difficulty arises because these arts resemble living organisms in that they begin at a certain point in time and move towards their end. The silence after they have concluded is like a death. Eliot then explains that the permanence of art is one of design rather than of duration. 'Reach/Into the silence' is contrasted with 'reach/The stillness'. The eternal now ('always now') of a work of art arises from the fact that its beginning and its end are in a continuous relationship, are both parts of a 'formal pattern'. Eliot then turns to another form of impermanence to which literature is especially prone. Words, themselves, the stuff of which literature is made, are continually subject to change because they are also the stuff of human speech. Withdrawal from society, however, creates other problems for the poet, the substitution of a dead or merely fanciful language for living speech. The first thirteen lines of this paragraph attempt to achieve stylistically the stasis which they describe. The lines move perpetually in their stillness through a very meagre use of verbs but mainly through a high degree of repetition, revolving the same words round and round, for instance, 'words' (three times), 'music' (twice), 'move' or 'moves' (three times), 'only' (five times), 'reach' (twice), 'stillness' or 'still' (four times), 'end' (three times), 'beginning' (three times), 'always' (twice). When Eliot turns from meditating on the fixity of art to comment on the unfixed nature of language the style reflects this changeableness. Repetition gives way to a highly varied vocabulary and this, together with a multiplicity of verbs, indicates the vitality of language. The association of words with the Logos or Word of St John's Gospel prepares for a transition from literary to religious and metaphysical concerns. It also looks back to the epigraph from Heraclitus at the beginning of 'Burnt Norton' and so ushers in the conclusion of the quartet.

The figure of the ten stairs is an image drawn from the writings of another St John, this time the Spanish mystic, St John of the Cross (see p.19). Like the reference to the Word it also links Eliot's aesthetic and religious concerns. In a design the complete pattern is still but the details which compose it are in movement, just as a staircase is still but its steps permit upward and downward movement. The stairs in St John's mystical treatise, *The Dark Night of the Soul*, is an image of the relationship between the soul and God and, therefore, allows Eliot to progress to a series of pronouncements on the nature of love and desire in relation to time and movement. Desire is unsatisfied and so moves towards love which causes it and is its goal. Love which is perfection is still and timeless but in the world of time it suffers the limitations of time. This section and the quartet as a whole then conclude with a moment in and out of time, a sudden flashback to the rose-garden scene of the opening. The vision occurs in time and space, 'now, here', but it also has a timeless quality, 'now, always'. This is one of those moments of heightened consciousness mentioned in 'Burnt Norton' II and in comparison to it the rest of time seems merely contemptible. The visionary moment is referred to as 'sudden' and 'quick' and its rapidity is caught, too, in the monosyllabic words, 'Quick, now , here, now . . .'. It interrupts the balanced clauses which preceded it and its 'hidden laughter' is made to contrast with the 'sad time' which follows it in the last two lines.

NOTES AND GLOSSARY:

The Word in the desert: a biblical allusion. Christ, referred to as the 'Word' or 'Logos' in the Gospel according to St John, went into the desert and fasted for forty days and afterwards was tempted by the devil

chimera: a fabled monster of Greek mythology, with a lion's head, a goat's body, and a serpent's tail. In ordinary modern usage it describes an unreal creature of the imagination, a mere wild fancy, an unfounded conception

the figure of the ten stairs: this refers to the ten steps of the ladder of love described by St John of the Cross in *The Dark Night of the Soul*, Book II, Chapter 19. St John calls his 'secret wisdom' a ladder, because a ladder is used for ascent and descent and communications from God both exalt and humble the soul. The saint's words are similar to those of Heraclitus in the second epigraph to 'Burnt Norton', '. . . upon this road to go down is to go up, and to go up, to go down'

'East Coker'

Title: East Coker is a small village near Yeovil on the borders of Dorset and Somerset in the south-west of England. It is the place where Eliot's ancestors lived and from which they emigrated to the New World around 1669. It, therefore, recalls an event in the Eliot family which was both an end and a beginning. East Coker is also reputed to be the place of origin of the family of Eliot's namesake, Sir Thomas Elyot (1499?–1546), author of the *Boke named the Governour* (1531), from which Eliot quotes in this quartet.

I. Although the opening line makes use of the terms 'beginning' and 'end' which had appeared repeatedly in 'Burnt Norton' V, 'East Coker' I is not a continuation of the first quartet. It, too, is concerned with time, but here time is regarded from a cyclic perspective and Eliot is concerned with the elemental rhythms of death and birth, not with the timeless moment. The visionary moment in 'East Coker' I, in fact, offers a historical rather than a personal epiphany. Eliot's focus is 'the turning world' rather than 'the still point'.

The first paragraph establishes the existence of a cyclic pattern or rhythm as a feature of life in time. It is full of references to decay and renewal, bringing together such opposites as 'beginning' and 'end', 'rise and fall', 'destroyed, restored', 'old' and 'new', 'live and die'. Eliot seems to be adopting Heraclitus's view of life as eternal flux, a ceaseless round of birth, death, growth and decay, in which death actually contributes to life. Heraclitus wrote: 'Fire lives in the death of earth, air lives in the death of fire, water lives in the death of air, and earth lives in the death of all water'. The phrase 'In succession' in line 1 introduces the idea of a cyclic process but it also has overtones of dynastic succession. The houses that rise and fall may be ordinary houses or dynasties. The latter reading ties in with the use of the motto of Mary, Queen of Scots. On her death, her son, James Stuart (1566–1625), became King James I of England and IV of Scotland and the Stuart dynasty replaced the Tudor. The phrase 'rise and fall' is altered to read 'live and die' in line 9 because Eliot is shifting attention from the buildings to the lives of their occupants. Similarly the paragraph, as a whole, moves from the outdoors to the domestic interior although here we are offered another instance of the workings of the cyclic process as in the concluding lines the natural world takes over from the human.

The style of this paragraph is deliberately rhythmic and incantatory. Clauses are carefully balanced, a half line to each, as in lines 5 and 6. The repetition of similar syntactic structures here, as well as in lines 9–11 and in lines 12 and 13, enacts in stylistic terms the cyclic repetitiveness which Eliot is describing. His style blends unobtrusively with that of Ecclesiastes in lines 10–12 and this biblical echo invests his utterance with authority.

The second paragraph is connected to the first by the use of the same opening sentence. The 'open field' and the 'stone' also look back to the first paragraph. Instead of a series of generalised reflections, however, we are here presented with a specific time and place. It is a summer afternoon and the 'deep lane' presumably leads into the village of East Coker. Eliot is preparing for the visionary experience of the next paragraph so he induces a state of semi-consciousness. The summer heat has an hypnotic effect. The phrase 'in the electric heat/Hypnotised' is placed in such a way as to refer to both the village and the speaker. Eliot emphasises the oppressive heat of the afternoon, the sultry atmosphere, the silence, the sleepiness of the flowers, the dim lighting. The scene is now set for the visionary moment.

The mention of the van and of electricity remind us that the time is the twentieth century but the vision we are shown in the third paragraph is of the 'open field' as it would have appeared in the sixteenth century. That it is the sixteenth century Eliot makes clear by quoting from Sir Thomas Elyot's *Boke named the Governour* and he underscores the point by retaining the original spelling. The dance, as Sir Thomas Elyot had seen, is an image both of the cycle of life and of the harmonious order of that cycle. Dancing couples man and woman as marriage does. The dance itself is cyclic. The dancers go 'Round and round' or are 'joined in circles'. Eliot then reminds us that these rustic dancers are long since dead, nourishing the life of the soil on which they had danced. In death as in life they participate in the cyclic rhythm of the universe. They are, therefore, connected through the word 'constellations' with the universal patterns of 'Burnt Norton' II, while the phrase 'rising and falling' and the reference to 'dung' (faeces) look back to the cyclical patterns of the first paragraph of 'East Coker' I. Eliot also reproduces the stylistic patterns of the first paragraph. This is especially noticeable in his re-echoing of Ecclesiastes in the series of phrases beginning 'The time of . . .'. Time is here being used in the musical sense of rhythm, 'keeping time', and Sir Thomas Elyot's sixteenth-century dance is being universalised to represent the cyclic harmonies of life in time. The allusion to Sir Thomas Elyot contributes, of course, to Eliot's theme of the temporal cycle. The twentieth-century Thomas Eliot returns to his ancestral village and sees the same vision as his sixteenth-century namesake, who was also a writer and may well have been an ancestor.

This third paragraph is concerned with the coupling aspect of dance; Eliot fashions a corresponding style based on the device of coupled phrases. One way of achieving this effect of stylistic coupling is through repetition, as is the case with 'If you do not come too close', 'Two and

two', 'Round and round', 'in their living in the living . . .', 'Keeping
time,/Keeping the rhythm . . .'. Occasionally he pairs associated words
such as 'pipe' and 'drum', 'man and woman', 'rising and falling', 'Eating
and drinking'. Sometimes alternatives are balanced, 'the hand or the
arm', 'Leaping' or 'joined', 'Rustically solemn or in rustic laughter'.
The paragraph concludes with a series of conjunctions, 'The time of . . .
and . . .', 'rising and falling', 'Eating and drinking', 'Dung and death'.

The movement of 'East Coker' I as a whole is in itself cyclic, since it
progresses in time through afternoon and midnight to the dawn of
another day. It ends with the image of a new beginning. The 'heat and
silence' of the day described in the second paragraph will be renewed.
Since this movement is full of opposites it concludes by turning from
the land and facing seawards. The destructive wind of the first para-
graph is now a dawn wind at sea. 'Wrinkles' is primarily an image of
the way in which the wind ruffles the water but the collocation of 'dawn'
and 'wrinkles' also has associations with youth and age. The action of
'East Coker' I has been set in the present day, in the sixteenth century,
and in the intervening years as well. It embraces both land and sea.
The movement ends, therefore, on a note of dislocation, 'I am here/Or
there, or elsewhere'. The cyclic effect of 'East Coker' I is completed
when Eliot concludes as he had started, 'In my beginning'.

NOTES AND GLOSSARY :

In my beginning is my end: a reversal of the motto embroidered on the
chair of state of Mary Queen of Scots (1542-87),
'En ma fin est mon commencement'. The quartet
ends with a straightforward rendering of the motto,
'In my end is my beginning'. Another possible
source is a sentence from Heraclitus: 'The begin-
ning and the end are common'. The phrase also
recalls a line in the final movement of 'Burnt Nor-
ton', 'And the end and the beginning were always
there'

there is a time . . . And a time for . . . And a time for: the syntactical con-
struction used here echoes the Bible, Ecclesiastes 3

The association of man and woman . . . concorde: the passage is adapted
from Sir Thomas Elyot's *Boke named the Gover-
nour*, Chapter 13. The opening paragraph of this
chapter reads :

It is diligently to be noted that the associatinge of
man and woman in daunsinge, they bothe obseru-
inge one nombre and tyme in their meuynges, was
not begonne without a special consideration, as

well for the necessarye coniunction of those two
persones, as for the intimation of sondry vertues,
whiche be by them represented. And for as moche
as by the association of a man and a woman in
daunsinge may be signified matrimonie, I coulde in
declarynge the dignitie and commoditie of that
sacrament make intiere volumes . . .

Further along we come upon the sentence:

In every daunse, of a moste auncient custome, there
daunseth together a man and a woman, holding
eche other by the hande or the arme, whiche be-
tokeneth concorde.

Eliot has preserved the archaic spelling of his source.
Sir Thomas Elyot's book has been described as the
earliest treatise on moral philosophy in the English
language

II. The short, rhymed lyric which opens this movement depicts a state
of universal chaos through a series of images of earth and sky. On earth
the seasons are confused. Winter is connected with spring and summer
and the flowers of these different seasons, spring snowdrops, summer
hollyhocks and winter roses, appear to bloom simultaneously. There
is war in the heavens, probably an echo of the Second World War.
Thunder imitates the sound of war chariots or armoured tanks, the
constellations and planets are in conflict, comets and satellite stars
suffer. The universe is hurtling to destruction by fire before the start of
the next glacial age. The image of the 'destructive fire', which receives
only a brief mention here, will be a key image in 'Little Gidding'. The
lyric consists of a series of images which amplify its main theme and
restate it in different ways.

Eliot repudiates this kind of poetry at the beginning of the next para-
graph, pronouncing it unsatisfactory, a roundabout and outdated
mode of expression. The poet's business is to attempt to come to terms
with words and with the meaning of experience rather than to indulge
in fanciful images. Eliot now begins to write in a direct, conversational
manner. Our attention is drawn to this stylistic change by the phrase 'to
start again'. Although this phrase is inserted with seeming casualness
through the use of parenthesis it will play a significant part in 'East
Coker' V where every attempt at writing is 'a wholly new start' and
'Home is where one starts from'. As in the preceding lyric Eliot begins
by asking questions. On this occasion, however, he is concerned with
human rather than with cosmic issues. What is being questioned is the

traditional view of old age as a time of serenity and wisdom. The conversational tone becomes flippant with the introduction of the internal rhymes 'receipt' and 'deceit' which also chime assonantally with 'bequeathing' and 'merely', as 'serenity' does with 'hebetude'. The serenity of age is equated with stupidity and its wisdom is dismissed as a collection of useless facts. The questioning tone yields to an authoritative tone. Eliot turns to the notion of pattern which had preoccupied him in 'Burnt Norton' V. Here he distinguishes between the pattern which experience may make us impose on events and the pattern of events themselves. Instead of allowing the past to influence our view of the present we should let the present revise our view of the past. Throughout this paragraph there is much bandying about of words associated with deceit ('deceived' (twice), 'deceit', 'falsified', 'undeceived', 'deceiving'), because Eliot is offering a 'new and shocking' exposure of traditional illusions about old age. Statement modulates into imagery with the allusion to the beginning of Dante's *Divine Comedy*, yet another fresh start. Eliot extends Dante's metaphor of being lost in a dark wood in middle age so that it embraces the whole of life. He then substitutes for the dark wood the more treacherous image of a marsh where monsters threaten and phosphorescent lights may lead one astray. Returning to a poetry of statement Eliot names the chief attribute of old age as fear rather than wisdom. Old age is afraid of passion, of attachment to anyone, even to God. True wisdom, for Eliot, consists in the self-abasement of humility, a state of being already advocated in 'Burnt Norton' III. The last two lines of this movement, which parody some lines from Robert Louis Stevenson's poem 'Requiem', are deliberately linked to 'East Coker' I by the reference to 'houses' and 'dancers' and to land and sea. 'Gone under' is a euphemism for 'dead' and this, together with the reminisicence of the title, 'Requiem', and such words as 'bequeathing' and 'dead secrets', discreetly reminds us that death follows old age. 'East Coker' II concludes with two powerful images of finality.

NOTES AND GLOSSARY:

Scorpion, Sun, Moon, Comets, Leonids: Eliot is describing a war in heaven which corresponds to the war on earth. Scorpio and Leo are signs of the zodiac. Scorpio is victorious over the sun in late autumn and the Leonids (meteors radiating from Leo) appear in mid-November three times a century

that destructive fire . . . ice-cap reigns: a forecast of the end of the world. It will be destroyed by fire and then a new ice age will begin

receipt: old-fashioned English for recipe or formula

hebetude: stupidity
In the middle . . . wood: an adaptation of the opening lines of Dante's *Divine Comedy* which read in translation:

> In the middle of the journey of our life
> I found myself in a dark wood,
> Having lost the straight path

grimpen: the first recorded use of the word is in Sir Arthur Conan Doyle's (1859–1930) *The Hound of the Baskervilles* (1902), 'Life has become like that great Grimpen Mire, with little green patches everywhere into which one may sink with no guide to point the track'. Eliot was an addict of Sherlock Holmes (the famous detective created by Conan Doyle)

The houses . . . under the hill: an ironic parody of two lines of the Scottish writer Robert Louis Stevenson's (1850–94) poem, 'Requiem':

> Home is the sailor, home from the sea,
> And the hunter home from the hill

III. In 'East Coker' II there had been several references to darkness but darkness is the dominant image in 'East Coker' III. The previous movement had begun with stellar conflict; this one begins in the dark empty spaces between the stars. It opens with the words of Milton's Samson, a blind man lamenting that he has lost all hope of light. Eliot then plunges the whole world into darkness. All the leaders of men with all their reliable sources of information are equally in the dark. A corpse-like numbness paralyses the society. The phrase, 'They all go into the dark' looks back to the last two lines of 'East Coker' II and also reverses Vaughan's famous line about his dead friends, 'They are all gone into the world of light'. Eliot appears to be as despairing as Milton's Samson at first but he then shows that darkness may be a positive rather than a negative condition. The obliteration of the normal world allows for an emphasis on the life of the soul. Darkness is now equated with that condition which St John of the Cross described as 'the dark night of the soul', a mystical state also advocated at this point in 'Burnt Norton'. As in 'Burnt Norton' III the individual may dissociate himself from the common fate of humanity. Eliot describes this mystical state of passive waiting for union with God in three up-to-date similes, one of which, the tube simile, recalls 'Burnt Norton' III. The first simile, drawn from the theatre, reveals how darkness can sometimes be an interval during which necessary changes occur. The audience in the theatre knowing this is content to wait in the dark. The second simile also concerns an interval, this time on an Underground train journey. Here the protagonists are frightened by inaction. The third simile employs the image of a patient who is etherised and, therefore, thinking of nothing. All these similes describe a state of suspense. The activity in each case is that of waiting upon an event. Eliot then applies the necessity of such waiting upon the event to the life of the soul. The 'dark night of the soul' is a method of arriving at experience of God or the One through successively discarding ideas which would limit the notion of his Being. If the soul remains completely passive without hope or love or thought then a spiritual transformation will take place. This is described in the paradoxical images, 'the darkness shall be the light, and the stillness the dancing'. The positive images of light and dancing are followed by a series of other positive sensuous images drawn from the natural world and, in particular, from the rose-garden of 'Burnt Norton' I. The suggestion of unseen delights and of echoes, as well as the reference to laughter, recalls the rose-garden. All such delights are dependent for their existence on the human condition and are inseparable, therefore, from the agony of death and birth.

In 'East Coker' III Eliot is again confronting the difficult task of writing a poetry of negation, describing a state which denies that life of the senses on which poets usually rely for their images. The disappearance of the sensuous is established in the opening lines with the triple repetition of 'dark' and 'vacant'. People and objects are listed only to be dispatched into darkness. The imagery then becomes funereal. The funeral is turned into a doubly negative occasion. It is 'nobody's funeral' and there is 'no one to bury'. The admonition to the soul is a dramatic device to enliven the passage. The three similes which follow permit Eliot to evoke images from normal human life and so provide a respite from total negativity. After the similes the admonition to the soul is renewed and Eliot again faces the problem of describing a state in which nothing whatever happens. He has recourse to the device of naming various possibilities only to dismiss them and he maintains a state of suspense through four references to the idea of waiting. Finally the suspense is over and a series of positive sensuous images appears. After this glimpse of joy Eliot feels able to risk another paragraph on the rewards of negativity. The private voice communing aloud with its own soul yields to a dogmatic public voice lecturing the reader. The style in this final paragraph is highly rhetorical, full of syntactical repetition. Its authority is derived from its reworking of a passage from St John of the Cross. This saint and mystic had been an unobtrusive presence throughout 'East Coker' III but in the final paragraph Eliot openly adopts his persona and speaks with the voice of the saint.

NOTES AND GLOSSARY:

O dark dark dark: quoted from John Milton's (1608–74) verse drama *Samson Agonistes* (1671). Samson is bewailing his blindness:

> O dark, dark, dark, amid the blaze of noon,
> Irrecoverably dark, total eclipse
> Without all hope of day . . .

vacant interstellar spaces: further on in the same speech from *Samson Agonistes* we come upon the lines:

> The sun to me is dark
> And silent as the moon,
> When she deserts the night
> Hid in her vacant interlunar cave.

In his essay on Milton Eliot refers to the use of the word 'interlunar' here as 'a stroke of genius'. 'Interstellar' refers to the dark spaces between the stars

They all go into the dark: an adaptation of a well-known line from the metaphysical poet Henry Vaughan's (1622–95) 'Ascension Hymn': 'They are all gone into the world of light'. Vaughan is writing about his dead friends. The presumption is that they have all gone to heaven. Eliot's viewpoint is negative and the people he mentions are not literally dead

Almanach de Gotha, Directory of Directors: directories which furnish particulars of public companies

Stock Exchange Gazette: a weekly bulletin of financial news

the darkness of God: refers to the 'dark night of the soul', a stage on the way to mystical union with God. St John of the Cross has written a poem on the subject and his two prose treatises are an exposition of it

In order to arrive there . . . in which you are not: the entire passage is based on the maxims of St John of the Cross in *The Ascent of Mount Carmel*, Book I, Chapter 13, which reads as follows:

> In order to arrive at having pleasure in everything,
> Desire to have pleasure in nothing.
> In order to arrive at possessing everything,
> Desire to possess nothing.
> In order to arrive at being everything
> Desire to be nothing.
> In order to arrive at knowing everything,
> Desire to know nothing.

In order to arrive at that wherein thou hast no
   pleasure,
Thou must go by a way wherein thou hast no
   pleasure.
In order to arrive at that which thou knowest not,
Thou must go by a way that thou knowest not.
In order to arrive at that which thou possessest not,
Thou must go by a way that thou possessest not.
In order to arrive at that which thou art not,
Thou must go through that which thou art not

IV. This is a Passion lyric treating of the fall of the human race through
Adam's sin and its redemption by Christ in the Crucifixion. The spiritual
malady of the human race is described in images of physical illness. The
poem is based on the Christian paradox that spiritual wholeness can
be achieved only through suffering and purgation. Eliot has modernised
this traditional Christian message by his use of up-to-date allegorical
images such as the surgeon, the fever chart, the ruined millionaire.

The 'wounded surgeon' of the first verse is Christ, often referred to
as the 'Divine Physician' in devotional literature. He is presented as
performing an operation in order to cure man's spiritual illness but he,
too, is wounded since he shared man's suffering by his Crucifixion.
'Compassion' literally means 'suffering with'. The 'dying nurse' is the
Church which mediates between the wounded Christ and the ailing
human race. Spiritual sickness results from God's curse on Adam. The
'ruined millionaire' is Adam who lost both spiritual and earthly riches
when he sinned against God. All his descendants have inherited his
disease of original sin so that the whole world is like a hospital. The
'absolute father' who cares for us is God who is omnipresent in the
universe. The fourth stanza depicts the progress of the disease through
chills and fever. It spreads throughout the body and infects the mind.
The 'mental wires', an image based on telegraph wires, refers to the
nerves. The chills and fevers are compared to the sufferings of purgatory.
Purgatory, in Christian belief, is a state in which souls, too imperfect to
be admitted to heaven after death, undergo further purification. The
purgatorial fire is finally transformed into an image of beauty, a mys-
tical rose. The last stanza begins by describing the Eucharist, the central
rite of Christian worship. The use of the adjectives 'dripping' and
'bloody' vividly conveys the idea of a sacrificial meal, the partaking of a
sacrificial victim. In spite of that frequent reminder of the Crucifixion
in the Eucharist, Christians forget that they are spiritually sick. The day
of the Crucifixion is known, of course, as Good Friday. Eliot enlivens
the familiar phrase by inverting it.

'East Coker' III had accustomed us to the paradoxes of Christianity.

Its concluding paragraph, in particular, consisted of a series of paradoxical statements. 'East Coker' IV is also riddled with paradox but here paradox is operating at an imagistic level. We read of a 'wounded surgeon', a 'dying nurse', 'frigid . . . fires'. 'Health' is described as a 'disease', dying as doing well, freezing as a method of becoming warm. The lyric ends by drawing attention to the commonplace paradox of referring to the day of the Crucifixion as Good Friday. The style of this poem is discussed in greater detail in the section entitled 'The lyrics', p.57.

V. Eliot's attempt to master his craft is the theme of the first paragraph. He is now in 'the middle way' described by Dante and referred to in 'East Coker' II. He has devoted the interval between the wars to constant experimentation. His struggles as a writer are depicted in military metaphors, each attempt a 'raid', with 'shabby equipment', his emotions behaving like 'undisciplined squads'. There is territory 'to conquer' and a 'fight to recover' it. Eliot regards writing as a series of adventures. The poet is not like an explorer discovering new territory, however, because the great writers of the past have already made all the discoveries. It only remains for the modern artist, despite the difficulties, to rediscover for his own age the literary skills that have been lost and found before. The emphasis is on effort rather than on achievement.

From literature considered as exploration we turn to the larger adventure of life. 'East Coker' had opened with a return to Eliot's ancestral and personal origins and it ends similarly. Home is seen as the place from which one begins life's journey as Eliot's ancestors had set out from the village of East Coker. Life becomes more complex as one proceeds because the accumulation of previous personal and ancestral experience is part of the texture of each moment. The poem, too, is continually modified by allusions to its own past. The opening sentence of this paragraph links life and literature, recalling as it does the phrases 'every attempt/Is a wholly new start' and 'each venture/Is a new beginning' from the first paragraph. The 'old stones' may be neolithic monuments or tombstones but they also recall the ruined houses of 'East Coker' I, as does the repetition of the phrase, 'there is a time for . . .'. Here there is a time both for experience and for the recollection of experience, for life outdoors and indoors. The photograph album is a collection of images of the past. True love is not confined by space or time, the 'here and now'. The attitude to old age is much more positive than it was in 'East Coker' II. Like the poet in the first paragraph old men should be explorers but the word has undergone a change of meaning and is now used in a spiritual sense. The journey now becomes the negative way of St John of the Cross, described in 'East Coker' III, although the phrase 'still and still moving' looks back to 'Burnt Norton'.

It is a journey to union with the One through darkness, deprivation and loneliness and it concludes in the vast desolation of the sea which traditionally has been associated in literature with the passage from life to eternity. We remember that there was sea imagery also at the conclusion of the first and second movements of this quartet and, of course, Eliot is also looking forward to the maritime setting of the next quartet, 'The Dry Salvages'. 'East Coker' V has a beginning, a middle and an end but these are not arranged as one might expect. It starts in the middle, as Dante did in the *Divine Comedy*, continues with an end and concludes with a beginning. The quartet, as a whole, is circular since its first and last words are, 'my beginning'. Its last sentence, however, is a triumphant reversal of its first.

In the final paragraph of 'East Coker' V Eliot mentions that the pattern of life becomes 'more complicated' as one grows older. This complexity is matched by the highly patterned style of the writing at this stage. Eliot begins by using near repetition for purposes of qualification as, for instance, 'Not the intense moment . . . But . . . every moment' and 'a lifetime . . . not the lifetime . . .'. This is succeeded by such near repetitions as '. . . . here and now cease to matter' and 'Here and there does not matter', and the two phrases beginning 'a time for . . .'. Then the repetition is reduced to one word as in 'still and still moving', the echo of 'union' in 'communion' and the repeated 'cry' of the penultimate line. In the concluding lines the pattern is obviously alliterative.

NOTES AND GLOSSARY:

in the middle way: another reference to the opening of Dante's *Divine Comedy*

l'entre deux guerres: (*French*) the period between the First and Second World Wars, that is, 1919–39

'The Dry Salvages'

Title: Eliot's note explains the location of the Dry Salvages. The poet's family went to the coast of Cape Ann (at Massachusetts in the United States) in the summer when he was a boy to escape from the heat of St Louis, Missouri.

I. The first movement of 'The Dry Salvages' makes use of the contrasting symbols of river and sea. The river is associated with the Mississippi beside which Eliot grew up and the sea with the New England coast where he spent his summers as a child. The first paragraph focuses on the role of the river in the life of primitive man and the progressive alienation from elemental nature which follows in the wake of progress.

Eliot begins by regarding the river as primitive man would have looked on it as a powerful god who has human moods but is beyond human control. To the early settlers the river serves as a natural boundary. Then it provides an unsafe means of transport to traders. Finally it is taken into consideration only by engineers. Cities are usually built near a river but it is no longer important to city-dwellers and so they forget its presence. The river, however, reminds them of its existence from time to time by flooding. Although modern men are too technologically sophisticated to think of the river as a god it remains a hostile force in their lives. Through a series of images the rhythm of the river is related to the rhythm of the cycle of life, to childhood, to sleep and waking, to spring flowering and autumn fruit, to times of day, such as evening and meal-times. Eliot's Introduction of 1950 to *Huckleberry Finn* (1884) by Mark Twain (Samuel Clemens, 1835-1910) helps to illuminate his presentation of the river in this passage:

> Mark Twain makes you see the River, as it is and was and always will be . . . As with Conrad,* we are continually reminded of the power and terror of Nature, and the isolation and feebleness of Man . . . Mark Twain is a native, and the River God is his God. It is as a native that he accepts the River God, and it is the subjection of Man that gives to Man his dignity. For without some kind of God, Man is not even very interesting.

Diction in the first paragraph veers between the prosaic and the romantic as Eliot presents different attitudes to the river. Phrases like 'a problem confronting' and 'The problem once solved' belong to the language of the business world, while lines 7 to 10 by contrast convey emotional urgency. The opening line, which introduces the idea of the river as a god, is apologetic and slackly colloquial, while the concluding four lines of the paragraph, in contrast, are taut and emphatically rhythmic.

The sea is depicted as altogether more vast and more incomprehensible than the river. It encompasses the whole world. It hints at a time that precedes human civilisation. It declares its superiority to the human race in the casual, offhand manner in which it throws back what it has destroyed. It has a multiple personality and is mysterious in its workings. Eliot passes by way of 'the briar rose' and 'the fir trees' from the landsman's to the sailor's point of view. The orchestrated music of the sea is now described, its different voices distinguished. These many voices are then gathered into the one voice of the tolling bell. Eliot is probably recalling the Metaphysical poet John Donne's (1571-1631) use of the tolling bell in the context of the sea:

*The novelist Joseph Conrad (1857-1924)

No man is an Island, entire of it self; every man is a piece of the Continent, a part of the main; if a Clod be washed away by the Sea, Europe is the less, as well as if a Promontory were, as well as if a Manor of thy friends or of thine own were; any man's death diminishes me, because I am involved in Mankind; And therefore never send to know for whom the bell tolls; It tolls for thee.

The sea represents eternity and this is contrasted with the pettiness of human calculations about time. A religious note is sounded at the conclusion of the passage by the quotation from the 'De Profundis' and by echoes of the doxology. Even the clanging of the bell which rounds off the paragraph has religious as well as musical connotations.

The section devoted to the sea begins with a series of precise visual images. A series of aural images follows and this is succeeded by a series of abstract images of time. The lines on time also emphasise the poverty and paltriness of human life which is described as a continuous process of mending and making do. The clang of the bell at the end with its echo of the earlier bell is a reminder of the ground swell of the eternal sea.

NOTES AND GLOSSARY:

ailanthus: a tree that grows in the southern states of America. Eliot referred to this and the 'long dark river', the Mississippi, as features of his childhood landscape

dooryard: an Americanism for the English 'back-yard'

horseshoe crab: king crab

algae: seaweed

seine: fishing-net

rote: a continuous roar made by waves dashing on a long, rocky coast. It indicates a change in the wind. The word is seldom heard outside New England

groaner: see Eliot's note

Ground swell: heavy sea caused by distant or past storm or earthquake

chronometers: time-measuring instruments used for navigation by astronomical sights at sea

the morning watch: 'watch' is a term used of a four-hour spell of duty on board ship. The phrase has religious connotations since it is used in Psalm 130, known as 'De Profundis'

is and was from the beginning: based on the doxology, a liturgical formula often used at the conclusion of a prayer: 'As it was in the beginning, is now, and ever shall be, world without end'

II. The lyric with which the second movement begins depicts the horror and boredom of human life in sea imagery. The three images in the first stanza portray destruction and death at the vegetable, inanimate and animal or human level, recalling, in particular, the way in which the sea 'tosses up our losses' on the beach. The annunciation at this point is written with a small initial letter so its religious overtones are subdued and it retains its primary meaning of message, here a message of disaster. The religious note is sounded but dismissed also in the phrase, 'unprayable prayer'. The first stanza is cast in the form of a question which the second stanza answers. Despair is confirmed here and life is depicted as a meaningless passing of time among the wreckage of belief. The third stanza is equally pessimistic. Old age with the faculties gradually failing is compared to a voyage in a slowly leaking boat waiting for the final summons of death. Under the metaphor of fishermen setting out on dangerous voyages Eliot pictures the lives of individual men, the sum of which makes history, in the fourth stanza. The repetitiveness and monotony of life are depicted again in images drawn from the lives of fishermen, in the fifth stanza. The conclusion would appear to be that there is no end to the wretchedness of the human lot since the final stanza circles round to repeat words and phrases from the first stanza with very little variation. At the last moment, however, we are offered a reprieve. The 'unprayable prayer' of the first stanza is modified to become a 'hardly, barely prayable/Prayer'. The Annunciation, now capitalised, refers to the announcement to the Virgin Mary that she was to be the Mother of God and so points to a new source of hope for the human race, a new beginning. The Virgin's prayer at the Annunciation is one of acceptance of a seemingly impossible role in life. The lyric is written in the form of a sestina. Its formal characteristics will be discussed later in the section on Lyrics.

Eliot now turns to a meditation on time from the perspective of middle age as in 'East Coker' V. He dismisses ways of regarding time in terms of chronology or progress as ways of dispossessing ourselves of the past. Instead he focuses on significant moments in the past which can be retrieved. These happy moments, sudden flashes of illumination, may be enjoyed uncomprehendingly at the time. When understanding comes later we relive these experiences on a higher plane of awareness. This applies to the historical as well as to the personal past. The primitive fears of our ancestors are not remote but are still within our reach. Just as happy moments can be retrieved so can moments of suffering, but this is truer of the agony of others than of our own. The wear and tear of living blunts our memory of the agony we ourselves have endured but friends' suffering is still vivid for us. The past is over in one sense but in another it is permanently accessible. Time is both a destroyer and a preserver. Eliot draws on the river and sea imagery of 'Dry

Salvages' I to illustrate his viewpoint. The river destroys things but it also preserves them in the sense that it transports them like cargo. The rock, like one of the Dry Salvages, is sometimes neutral but is also a destroyer and preserver. It can act in a positive capacity as a seamark in fair weather or in a negative capacity as a destroyer of unsuspecting craft in foul weather.

NOTES AND GLOSSARY:

annunciation: announcement

hauling: in the nautical sense, this means turning a ship's course

erosionless: not suffering the effects of erosion, gradual destruction or wearing away. Eliot coined this word for the sake of the rhyme

Annunciation: when used with capital 'A' as here, this indicates the announcement of the Incarnation made by the Angel Gabriel to the Virgin Mary

Prayer of the one Annunciation: this refers either to the angelus (see note p.39) or else to Mary's prayer of acceptance which it incorporates, 'Be it done unto me according to Thy Word'

attrition: friction, wearing out. In theological terms this can mean sorrow for sin

Time the destroyer . . . preserver: this echoes a line from the English romantic poet Shelley's (1792–1822) 'Ode to the West Wind' in which he addresses the wind as 'Destroyer and preserver'

the bite in the apple: this refers to the biblical story of Eve's eating of the forbidden fruit which caused God to punish the human race

halcyon day: calm day, originally used of the fourteen days about the winter solstice

III. In the third movement Eliot ponders the relationship between present and future and here he introduces the scriptures of the East to give his views authority and universality. The fundamental concept that Eliot takes from the *Bhagavadgita* is that of disinterested action: 'To work alone thou hast the right, but never to the fruits thereof'. Man must preserve 'an even mind in success or failure, for evenness of mind is called "yoga"'. Eliot applies the concept of 'yoga' to the problem of life in time. Evenness of mind makes one indifferent to past and future. This idea is translated into a series of images in which the future is described in images usually attributed to the past, images of fading and regret, of flowers pressed between the pages of an unopened book. Such an equation of past and future brings to mind the stairs or ladder of St John of the Cross ('Burnt Norton' V) which allows both upward and downward movement. Eliot also reverts to the sickness imagery of 'East Coker' IV to overturn an old proverb about the future: Time heals all wounds. The image of passengers from 'Burnt Norton' III reappears but these passengers are no longer in the Underground but on a long train journey or sea voyage. They are moving forward but not travelling from past to future. The journey is used here as an image of a continuous present not involved with past or future. The travellers should therefore achieve the state of 'yoga' and regard past and future with indifference. This renders them fit to receive the message of Krishna. Eliot, however, alters this message. He goes beyond the concern for the individual soul shown by Krishna to a sense of communal responsibility, a concern for the impact of 'yoga' on the lives of others. He also gives the notion of 'the time of death' an altogether wider application by equating it with every living moment. It is significant that Krishna's advice to Arjuna is given on the field of battle since Eliot is writing these lines in 1941, during the Second World War. The latter part of this movement from line 26 onward is in quotation marks because it purports to be a message to the voyagers uttered by a mysterious voice in the ship's rigging. The device Eliot employs here recalls the English Romantic poet Coleridge's (1772–1834) use of 'voices in the air', in 'The Rime of the Ancient Mariner' (1798), to convey information to the Ancient Mariner during his voyage. The way in which the descanting voice is described also recalls the English Romantic poet Keats's (1795–1821) description in 'Ode on a Grecian Urn' (1819) of pipes that play 'not to the sensual ear' but 'to the spirit ditties of no tone'. At the conclusion of the movement the message is addressed to both voyagers and seamen. The reference to seamen and to death by water looks back to the first and second movements of 'The Dry Salvages' and forward to its fourth movement. At the end Eliot reiterates his message in two brief, balanced phrases, 'Not fare well, / But fare forward'. Disinterested action (faring forward) is what counts, not successful action (faring well). Since this is the conclusion of the movement and since he is addressing travellers Eliot exploits the pun on 'goodbye' in using the words 'fare well'.

NOTES AND GLOSSARY:

Krishna:	great deity of later Hinduism, worshipped as an incarnation of Vishnu
Royal Rose:	the reference is to the Wars of the Roses, the fifteenth-century civil wars in England between Yorkists, whose emblem was a white rose, and Lancastrians, whose emblem was a red rose

lavender:	the scented flowers and stalks of this plant are laid among linens which are put by for future use
time is no healer:	a reversal of the proverb: 'Time heals all wounds'
descanting:	a musical term for a melodic independent treble accompaniment
'on whatever sphere . . . death':	Eliot is quoting from the *Bhagavadgita*, Chapter VII, entitled 'The Life Everlasting'. Krishna is replying to Arjuna's question, 'and at the time of death how many of those who have learned self-control come to the knowledge of Thee?' Eliot has omitted the concluding words of Krishna's sentence. In full it reads: 'On whatsoever sphere of being the mind of a man may be intent at the time of death, thither will he go'
Arjuna:	the great warrior-hero in the *Bhagavadgita*

IV. The lyrical fourth movement of 'The Dry Salvages' takes the form of an address but this time it is a prayer to the Virgin Mary in her role as 'Stella Maris', patron of sailors. Each stanza opens with a similar formal invocation, 'Pray for', 'Repeat a prayer also on behalf of', 'Also pray for'. The first formal address introduces a prayer for all sailors, for fishermen, merchant seamen, and pilots. The repetition of 'those' links all these different categories. In the second stanza the prayer is for the bereaved womenfolk of the seamen. The quotation from Dante places the Virgin in a familial context. The fact that she is both a mother and daughter and the mother of a dead son connects her with the women. In Dante's *Paradiso*, too, she is addressed by St Bernard as man's most powerful intercessor in heaven. The third formal address to Mary is for the shipwrecked. This stanza is linked to the first by the change of tense from 'those who are in ships' to 'those who were in ships'. The structure of this last stanza is also modelled on that of the first in that it consists of a series of parallel constructions, 'in ships', 'on the sand', 'in the sea's lips', 'or in the dark throat', 'or wherever . . .'. The lyric closes with a reference to the angelus which is 'the prayer of the one Annunciation' mentioned in 'The Dry Salvages' II. The sound of the sea bell associates the angelus with the 'tolling bell' rung by the 'Ground swell' in 'The Dry Salvages' I.

NOTES AND GLOSSARY:

Lady, whose shrine . . . promontory:	Eliot had in mind particularly the shrine of Notre Dame de la Gard, high up over-looking the Mediterranean at Marseilles. However, there are many such shrines to the Virgin Mary in her role as 'Star of the Sea' and patron of sailors

Figlia del tuo figlio: (*Italian*) from the first line of the final canto of Dante's *Paradiso* where the famous French ecclesiastic St Bernard (1090-1153) prays to Mary on Dante's behalf, concerning her role in aiding the spirit who would attain the Divine Vision. The literal translation is 'Daughter of your son'

angelus: prayer commemorating the Incarnation, said by Roman Catholics at morning, noon and sunset, at the sound of a bell

V. This movement begins with a catalogue of the various ways in which men try to distract or comfort themselves, especially in times of personal trouble or of universal disaster such as the Second World War. In particular, they turn to all kinds of fortune-tellers since their sole concern is with life in time. The frivolity of their attitude is emphasised by the fact that the war is referred to in terms of Christ's prophecy of the end of the world. This biblical reference also permits Eliot to make the transition to the life of the saint for purposes of contrast with the lives of ordinary men. Only the saint is interested in the relationship of time and the timeless. The saint's concern with a timeless dimension is an attitude rather than a professional role, a total sacrifice of the self out of love for God. The only escape from time and the self experienced by the majority of men is a fleeting recognition of beauty in a remembered scent, a flash of lightning, a waterfall, a piece of music in which one becomes absorbed. Such illuminations are momentary and the remainder of one's life has to be spent in a state of routine religious asceticism. The real intersection of the timeless with time, which we cannot fully comprehend, is the Incarnation. The union of time and the timeless, which seemed impossible, occurred when God became man. God is visualised as the Unmoved Mover participating in the world of action. For human beings to act rightly is to be unconcerned with temporal things, to achieve 'yoga', to be unlike the anxious women of 'The Dry Salvages' I. Most people aspire to this way of life rather than actually achieve it. Success must be measured in terms of effort rather than of achievement. The most we can hope is that our efforts will bear fruit in others' lives, a return to the preoccupation of 'The Dry Salvages' III.

NOTES AND GLOSSARY:
Mars: Roman god of war
report . . . the sea monster: this refers to journalists' articles on the Loch Ness monster, a way of distracting newspaper readers from more serious issues. Loch Ness, the largest lake in Scotland, is said to be inhabited by a monster—a matter much publicised in the 1930s

horoscope: observation of the sky and planets at a certain time, especially at a person's birth, in order to foretell the future

haruspicate: consult the haruspex, the augur, a Roman religious official, who foretold the future by examining the entrails of sacrificed animals

scry: to use the crystal in crystal-gazing, another method of seeing into the future

sortilege: divination by lots. Again a method of arriving at foreknowledge

pentagrams: five-pointed stars formed by producing the sides of pentagons (five-sided figures) both ways until they intersect. The pentagram was regarded as a mystic symbol

barbituric acids: acids from which various hypnotic and sedative drugs are derived

distress of nations and perplexity: quoted from the Bible, Luke 21, in which Christ prophesies the end of the world: 'And there shall be signs in the sun, and in the moon, and in the stars; and upon earth distress of nations, with perplexity . . .'

Incarnation: when capitalised it refers to God's assumption of human form

daemonic: inspired, of supernatural genius or impulses

chthonic: dwelling in or beneath the surface of the earth

reversion: return of what is left after death to the grantor or his heirs

---

'Little Gidding'

Title: Little Gidding is a village in Huntingdonshire where in 1626 Nicholas Ferrar established a Christian community of thirty-five to forty persons of both sexes and all ages. The community, which was based on the idea of the Christian family, combined regular religious devotions with intellectual and manual labours and provided a social service for the neighbourhood. King Charles I (1625–49) visited the community at Little Gidding in 1633 and in 1642. In May 1646, after the final defeat of his cause at Naseby, the king made his way there, looking for refuge. This time he came at night, a broken king on his way north to give himself up to the Scots. After the defeat of the Royalist cause in 1646 Parliamentary troops sacked the house and church and the community was dispersed.

I. The first paragraph introduces midwinter spring, a season which is in the natural cycle but which is also 'its own season', which is in time and yet 'Sempiternal'. It is a season of brightness characterised by brief but intense illuminations, for instance, 'the short day is brightest', 'The brief sun flames the ice', 'A glare that is brightness in the early afternoon'. It is also a season of opposites, poised between cold and heat, between pole and tropic, frost and fire, flame and ice, external cold and the heart's heat. The spiritual season of the second sentence corresponds to mid-winter spring. It, too, is a time of brief but keen illumination, of a 'glow more intense' than burning, of 'pentecostal fire'. It is also a time of opposites, of fire in the dark time, of melting and freezing. The natural season was 'windless' and the spiritual season also has 'no wind'. Like spring the spiritual season is a time of growth but it is the soul's sap which is rising. Similarly the bloom of midwinter spring is not a natural bloom which will bud and fade but snow which is outside the cycle of birth and death. 'Covenant' is a biblical word which conjures up God's compact with man in the Old Testament so that the phrase 'time's covenant' has both temporal and religious associations. The first paragraph is constructed on a tension of opposites. Natural images are used to gesture towards spiritual realities, to lend substance to the insubstantial. Eliot is describing a state of being which is in time but not of time, just as later at the end of the movement he will locate Little Gidding 'in England and nowhere'.

The first paragraph concludes by pointing towards summer. The second is set in summer when May blooms have replaced the 'transitory blossom/Of snow'. A series of five conditional clauses lends an air of tentativeness to this paragraph. The 'way', the 'route', the 'place' of departure, the purpose of the 'journey' are all left vague and unspecified. Little Gidding itself consists of two structural shells or husks, a façade and a tombstone. The purpose of the pilgrimage will come as a special revelation to each individual pilgrim. Although he is dealing with uncertainties Eliot succeeds in attaining a sense of authorial purposefulness by stylistic means. The passage is bound together by a series of rhetorical repetitions. The opening phrase, 'If you came . . .', occurs four times. Two clauses begin 'you would be likely to . . .' and 'It would be the same . . .', while the clause 'what you came for' also recurs. Words such as 'may', 'way', 'end', 'purpose' and 'fulfil' are repeated. The concrete reality of Little Gidding is affirmed at the end of the paragraph by locating it 'now and in England' by contrast with a series of other vaguely situated and unnamed shrines.

The repetition of the phraseology of the second paragraph at the beginning of the third has an incantatory value. Eliot's use of the journey image is similar to his earlier use of the mystical dark night of the soul. A process of spiritual adventure is being described. Its end is prayer, communication with God. Once again Eliot is forsaking the world of

'Sense and notion', on which poets usually rely, to achieve a higher communication which transcends the syntax and sound of language. The image of the pentecostal fire looks back to the first paragraph. The tongues of fire endow holy men, such as those who lived at Little Gidding, with strange powers of speech. The 'communication/Of the dead', however, also anticipates the encounter with the compound poet ghost in the next movement so that the language of prayer and the language of poetry are associated. In the final two lines of the second paragraph Little Gidding had been situated 'Now and in England' and thereby given a specific location 'in place and time'. In the final two lines of the last paragraph its existence is given in addition a transcendental dimension with the reintroduction of the idea of the 'timeless moment', first mentioned in 'Burnt Norton'. The 'timeless moment' there was not specifically religious as it is here. Little Gidding as a religious shrine represents the intersection of the timeless with time. It exists on two planes of awareness simultaneously. It is both in and out of place ('Is England and nowhere') and in and out of time ('Never and always'). Perhaps because he is dealing with spiritual matters which cannot be verified but which he believes to be true Eliot's tone and syntax become dogmatic and assertive and the final paragraph consists of a series of instructions and authoritative pronouncements.

NOTES AND GLOSSARY:

Sempiternal: a rhetorical word for 'eternal'

pentecostal: adjective from Pentecost. The reference is to the Bible, Acts 2:1–5: 'When the day of Pentecost had come, they [the apostles] were all together in one place. And suddenly a sound came from heaven like the rush of a mighty wind, and it filled all the house where they were sitting. And there appeared to them tongues as of fire, distributed and resting on each one of them. And they were all filled with the Holy Spirit and began to speak in other tongues, as the Spirit gave them utterance'. Images based on this biblical story will recur throughout 'Little Gidding'

covenant: a compact or agreement. In the Bible the word is used of the compact between God and the Israelites

generation: begetting or being begotten

Zero: Eliot probably has in mind the absolute zero of physics, the point in terms of temperature at which the particles whose motion constitutes heat would be at rest

voluptuary: given up to luxury and sensual gratification

broken king: see note on the title, p.40

places/Which also are the world's end: Eliot later identified these places. Those 'at the sea jaws' are the monastic settlements on the islands of Iona, in Scotland, and Lindisfarne, in Northumberland, associated with the Irish missionary and abbot St Columba (*c*.521–97) and the English monk and bishop St Cuthbert (*c*.635–687), respectively. The 'dark lake' is Glendalough, the hermitage of the Irish monk St Kevin (d.618 or 622) in County Wicklow, Ireland. The 'desert' is the Thebaid where St Antony (*c*.250–*c*.350), the first Christian monk, and his hermits retired to fast and pray, and the 'city' is the Italian city of Padua, home of the other St Anthony (1195–1231), a Franciscan monk

tongued with fire: a pentecostal image

II. Images from earlier quartets are woven into the beautiful lyric on destruction and death with which this movement opens. The first stanza is reminiscent of the first movement of 'East Coker', in particular, although 'burnt', 'roses' and 'dust' recall 'Burnt Norton'. 'Ash', 'house', 'wainscot' and 'mouse' all appear in the first movement of 'East Coker' I, but there change and decay were attributed to the passage of time while here they are due to 'death by air', the London Blitz. Eliot has remarked how 'during the Blitz the accumulated debris was suspended in the London air for hours after a bombing' and then 'would slowly descend and cover one's sleeve and coat with a fine white ash'. After the bombing all that is left of the story of some people's lives, of the houses where they lived, is a cloud of dust. This stanza also seems to be based on those familiar phrases from the burial service, 'Ashes to ashes and dust to dust'. The second stanza evokes the central image of 'The Dry Salvages'. Here water destroys the earth in two ways, by flooding or drought. The vanity of all human effort is mocked by the ease with which natural forces can destroy it. Eliot uses 'parched' and 'eviscerate' to connect the soil and the human body. The key ideas and images of the previous two stanzas are brought together in the third. Both town and country suffer and at the end of the stanza so do religious foundations, which reminds one of the destruction of Little Gidding. Death in this lyric is linked with the four elements, air, earth, water and fire, and these are given a position of emphasis at the conclusion of the three stanzas. The lyric also versifies a sentence of Heraclitus on the reconciliation of opposites which constitutes the flux of life: 'Fire lives in the death of air, and air in the death of fire; water lives in the death of earth, and earth in the death of water'.

The second section of this movement takes the form of a colloquy between Eliot and a 'compound ghost', modelled on Dante's encounter with Brunetto Latini in the *Divine Comedy* (*Inferno* XV). This section begins as the preceding lyric had begun in the time after an air-raid. For the landscape of hell and purgatory in which Dante spoke with the dead, Eliot has substituted the streets of wartime London at dawn between the departure of the last bomber and the sounding of the All Clear. The 'dark dove with the flickering tone' is a bomber plane, an image which anticipates 'Little Gidding' IV. The visionary figure whom Eliot encounters, although partly based on Yeats, is not to be identified with any one particular 'dead master' since he is a 'compound ghost'. The greeting 'What are *you* here' is an imitation of Dante's cry of horror when he discovered Brunetto Latini in hell, 'Siete vos qui, ser Brunetto'. Eliot substituted an italicised 'you' for the poet's name to convey an air of familiarity without mentioning any specific name. The two figures walk together like two air-raid wardens on patrol. The 'dead master' is unwilling to discuss his 'thoughts and theory' on the grounds that his work is now outdated as each new year demands a new mode of utterance. This accords with the view expressed by Eliot in 'East Coker' V. However, because London burning is so like hell or purgatory the ghost feels sufficiently at ease to speak. The dead poet who revisits the streets of London and whose body has been left on a distant shore is thought to be Yeats who had lived in London for many years and had been buried at Roquebrune in the south of France in January 1939. The adaptation of Mallarmé's line which follows balances the reference to Yeats to preserve the idea of the ghost as 'compound'. The description of 'the gifts reserved for age' looks back to an earlier passage on the same subject in 'East Coker' II. Old age is presented here with the kind of honesty for which Eliot had praised Yeats. Its first limitations are bodily decay and the disappearance of sensual delights. The presentation of old age at this point also resembles Milton's melancholy picture of it:

> Thou must outlive
> Thy youth, thy strength, thy beauty, which will change
> To withered weak and gray; thy Senses then
> Obtuse, all taste of pleasure must forgoe,
> To what thou hast . . .

Secondly, the wisdom of old age is regarded as making one acutely aware of human folly but powerless to prevent it. The word 'laceration' here recalls the epitaph on Dean Swift's (1667-1745) tomb and the Irish poet W.B. Yeats's (1865-1939) poem, 'Swift's Epitaph'. The Latin epitaph in St Patrick's Cathedral, Dublin, where the writer Swift is buried, reads:

Hic depositum est Corpus
IONATHAN SWIFT s.t.d.
Hujus Ecclesiae Cathedralis
        Decani,
Ubi saeva Indignatio
        Ulterius
Cor lacerare nequit.
        Abi Viator
Et imitare, si poteris,
Strenuum pro virili
Libertatis Vindicatorem
Obiit 19° Die Mensis Octobris
A.D. 1745 Anno Aetatis 78.

Yeats's poem reads:

Swift has sailed into his rest;
Savage indignation there
Cannot lacerate his breast.
Imitate him if you dare,
World-besotted traveller; he
Served human liberty.

The last gift is a reliving of past experience in the light of a later knowledge that exposes one's earlier faults and failings. For all these reasons the honour and approval accorded to old age act as irritants and life becomes more unbearable unless one achieves harmony and balance through purification in purgatorial fire. This anticipates 'Little Gidding' IV. The images of fire and dancing are common to Eliot and Yeats. In particular, they remind us of Yeats's poem on old age, 'Sailing to Byzantium':

O sages standing in God's holy fire
As in the gold mosaic of a wall,
Come from the holy fire, perne in a gyre,
And be the singing-masters of my soul.

After his speech the ghost bids farewell. The disappearance, in Shakespeare's *Hamlet*, of the ghost of Hamlet's father who 'faded on the crowing of the cock' is here updated by Eliot whose ghost fades on the blowing of the siren that sounds the All Clear.

Dante had written the *Divine Comedy* in *terza rima*, an Italian verse form composed of tercets which are not separate stanzas because each is joined to the one preceding and the one following by a common rhyme, that is, aba, bcb, cdc . . . . In this passage, written in imitation of Dante's style, Eliot has substituted an alternation of masculine and feminine endings for the alternating rhymes of *terza rima* and contented himself with an occasional half-rhyme. The first eight lines are devoted, ostensibly, to an elaborate definition of context, each phrase being introduced by a word indicative of time or place, for instance, 'in', 'before', 'near', 'at', 'after', 'while', 'over', 'where', 'between', 'whence'. There are references to 'hour', 'morning', 'night' and to a place 'between three districts'. The main clause 'I met one' is thus delayed and given more impact because of the suspense. Further inspection reveals that Eliot's precision about time and place is illusory. The hour is 'uncertain', the place is vaguely situated and the opening lines contain such paradoxes as 'the ending of interminable' and 'the recurrent end of the unending'. The note of paradox is continued in the description of the ghost, 'loitering and hurried', and contributes to the deliberate vagueness of the encounter: '"What are *you* here?"/Although we were not.' The conversation between poet and ghost is strongly reminisicent of such exchanges in the *Divine Comedy*. The phrases 'I said' and 'And he', for instance, recall Dante's 'Io dissi' and 'ed egli a me'. When questioning his guides, Virgil, Statius, Matilda and Beatrice, Dante always adopts a humble and attentive tone and Eliot displays a similar courtesy in his questioning. The ghost's speech is balanced and formal, occasionally ritualistic as, for example, in the allusion to the Lord's Prayer, 'and pray they be forgiven'. The description of 'the gifts reserved for age' is highly rhetorical. It has a tripartite structure, the third part of which has a tripartite syntactical structure and contains a triple repetition of the word 'done'.

NOTES AND GLOSSARY:

the dark dove with the flickering tongue: a bomber plane. The Holy Ghost is depicted traditionally in the form of a dove

brown baked features: based on the description of Brunetto Latini in Dante's *Inferno* XV. The adjective 'brown' approximates to the Italian *'Brunetto'*, and the rest is a translation of *'lo cotto aspetto'*

compound ghost: ghost of several persons simultaneously

To purify the dialect of the tribe: an adaptation of a line from Mallarmé's *'Le Tombeau d'Edgar Poe'*, *'Donner un sens plus pur aux mots de la tribu'*

that refining fire: Dante places the poet Arnaut Daniel (*c*.1180–1210) in a refining fire in *Purgatorio* XXVI

III. The image of the hedgerow, remembered from 'Little Gidding' I, is sustained throughout the first sentence so that the three attitudes of attachment, detachment and indifference are presented as natural growths. In particular, Eliot uses nettle imagery to point to resemblances and differences between these three attitudes. Indifference, that neither stings nor bears a flower, is placed between selfish love that stings and unselfish love that bears a white flower. Eliot continues by pointing out that memory purifies love by freeing it from desire which is a form of attachment. Love, even when it is love of country, begins with attachment but with the passage of time love is purified of this selfish element.

From this reflection on individual lives Eliot turns to the patterns of lives in history. A detached view of the past enables us to use it rather than be enslaved by it. Private enthusiasms for particular 'faces and places' yield to a more universal perspective, that of God, as revealed to Dame Julian of Norwich. According to Dame Julian's thirteenth revelation, God recognises the presence of evil in the universe but reassures us that 'All shall be well'. Eliot now focuses his attention once again on Little Gidding and on the historical period in which the religious community flourished, the time of the Civil War which saw the defeat and death of King Charles I, Laud and Strafford, among many others. As Eliot writes, England is again at war. To celebrate the dead, however, is not to summon back the past, to call up the ghost of earlier faction fighting, such as the Wars of the Roses. Those who fought to determine how England should be governed are all united ironically under the silent government of death. The living are the heirs of both the victors and the vanquished. The defeated, such as the community at Little Gidding, who defended the Royalist cause and suffered under the Roundheads, have left behind the symbol of a life of detachment which found fulfilment in death. The movement ends with a repetition of some phrases from Dame Julian's thirteenth revelation quoted earlier in the passage. To this Eliot has added an adaptation of a line from her fourteenth revelation: 'I am Ground of Thy Beseeching'. The movement then reaches the conclusion that all shall be well if we live a life of detachment and prayer. By contrast with the colloquial manner of the previous movement this one is assertive in tone and full of abstractions. Its authoritative statements blend unobtrusively with the pronouncements of Dame Julian.

NOTES AND GLOSSARY:

The live and the dead nettle: the dead nettle is of the family of flowering plants of which the white dead nettle is one of the commonest. It closely resembles the stinging nettle and is frequently found growing along with it

Sin is Behovely: this and the following two lines are adapted from the anchorite and mystical writer Dame Julian of Norwich's (c.1342–1413) *Revelations of Divine Love*. She received sixteen revelations in the year 1373. Eliot's lines are based on lines from the thirteenth revelation reading: 'Sin is behovabil, but all shall be well, and all shall be well, and all manner of thing shall be well'. Dame Julian is probably the greatest of the medieval English mystics. Eliot's nonce-word 'behovely' means useful or necessary

the strife which divided them: the Civil War, 1642–51

a king at nightfall: see note on the title, p.40

three men, and more, on the scaffold: the three were King Charles I, Archbishop Laud, and the English statesman Thomas Wentworth, Earl of Strafford (1593–1641). Nicholas Ferrar was ordained deacon by Laud

one who died blind and quiet: the Puritan poet, Milton, died 'blind and quiet' after the Commonwealth had failed. Eliot wrote of this period: 'It is not insignificant that the monarch who gives his name to the age is dignified with the style of martyr. On all sides, it was an age of lost causes, and unpopular names, and forsaken beliefs, and impossible loyalties . . .'

'ring . . . backward' and 'follow . . . drum': Eliot referred to the romantic Bonnie Dundee period effect of this part of the poem so he seems to be recalling some lines from the Scottish poet and novelist Sir Walter Scott's (1771–1832) famous song in *The Doom of Devorgoil*, II.ii:

Dundee he is mounted, he rides up the street,
The bells are rung backward, the drums they are beat . . .

the spectre of a Rose: this refers to the Wars of the Roses, already recalled in 'The Dry Salvages' III. Eliot also had in mind the Russian ballet, *Le Spectre de la Rose*. There may also be a reminiscence of Sir Thomas Browne's (1605–82) phrase, 'raise up the ghost of a Rose', from *The Garden of Cyrus* (1658) V

the ground of our beseeching: in her fourteenth revelation, on prayer, Julian of Norwich heard the words, 'I am Ground of thy Beseeching'

IV. The two-stanza structure of this lyric is peculiarly suitable since Eliot's theme is the dual nature of suffering.

The dove, traditionally associated with the Holy Spirit who descended on the Apostles in the form of tongues of fire, is here an enemy aircraft whose tongues, nevertheless, offer a kind of deliverance from sin. This is an amplification of an image which occurs in 'Little Gidding'

II. The noun 'discharge' is used in a double sense. It describes a burst of gunfire from the fighter plane but also has the legal sense of acquittal, of freeing one from a charge held against him, an image of redemption. As in 'East Coker' IV the basic idea is that suffering has to be undergone by the Christian if spiritual deliverance is to be achieved. Physical suffering in this world saves from hell fire in the next.

The second stanza opens with a question which relates to the first. The Holy Spirit is here given his traditional identification with love. Love is responsible for the devastation of the Second World War. In Greek mythology Hercules was condemned to wear a shirt of flame from which he escaped only by mounting his own funeral pyre, an image which perfectly conveys the idea of being 'Consumed by either fire or fire'. Like the first stanza the second also ends with a choice between two alternative forms of suffering. In the second stanza the choice is between regarding suffering as the fire of evil, or the fire of love redeeming through purgation. The repetition of 'pyre' and 'fire' in the concluding couplet of each stanza underscores the surface similarity of the two forms of suffering. The couplets in both stanzas are also linked through the use of the same rhyme. Suffering is unpleasant no matter what the cause or the way in which one regards it. Repetition, however, emphasises the fact that the same suffering can be considered under two different aspects, as physical torment or as spiritual purification.

V. As befits the closing movement of a long poem this one is full of echoes from the earlier quartets. The opening lines, for instance, recall the meditation on time in 'Burnt Norton' and 'East Coker'. 'End' is here used in its usual ambiguous sense of purpose and conclusion. 'The end is where we start from' is a variation on the phrase 'Home is where one starts from' ('East Coker' V). As is the case with the fifth movement of each quartet this one, too, is concerned with words, so that the philosophical preoccupation with 'beginning' and 'end' is given a literary bias. Here the image of home is used to establish a sense of common context. Every word must be carefully chosen if the phrase or sentence is to sound right. When no word is out of key, perfect harmony is established as in a dance. The reference to 'dancing' looks back to 'Burnt Norton', 'East Coker' and 'Little Gidding' II. Every poem is an epitaph in the sense that its subject is what is past, or as the 'compound ghost' expresses it: 'Last season's fruit is eaten'. The word 'epitaph' introduces the idea of death. Life is seen as a process that culminates in death whether it be death on the scaffold as in the case of King Charles I, Strafford and Laud, or death by fire as for Hercules and for the victims of air-raids, or death by water as in 'The Dry Salvages', or the quiet consummation and unrenowned graves of the villagers of East Coker.

As 'East Coker' demonstrated, however, death is a new beginning.

The image of the rose from the beginning of *Four Quartets* had been associated with life in time and the yew tree with death and burial. Here the two are equated in time. This reconciliation, occurring as it does half-way through the final movement, anticipates the image of union at the conclusion of the poem. Throughout *Four Quartets* Eliot had been preoccupied with the idea of the timeless moment, the intersection of the timeless with time. God operates through time so history is now presented as a pattern of such moments. The visit to Little Gidding is one such moment. Although it is a visit to a particular place at a particular season and time (a winter's afternoon) it is also an epiphany of England and its history. The quotation from *The Cloud of Unknowing* which separates the first from the second paragraph serves as a reminder of God's presence in the universe, attracting all things to Himself.

In the concluding paragraph Eliot weaves a pattern of moments from the history of his own poem. He begins by turning again to the image of exploration from 'East Coker' V. Exploration is connected with the theme of beginnings and endings with which he had introduced this movement since the end of exploration in this poem is to arrive at one's beginning. Exploration is then connected to the beginning of human life in the Garden of Eden and to the beginning of *Four Quartets* with the image of the 'remembered gate' from 'Burnt Norton'. Through this gate Eliot travels back to revisit other images from his long poem, the Mississippi river, the waterfall and the sea from 'The Dry Salvages', the children hidden in the foliage and the voice of the bird ('Quick now, here, now, always') from 'Burnt Norton' I and V. Over and over again in the quartets Eliot had dwelt on the need for asceticism in order to achieve union with God. At this point his poem moves towards the moment of union through total sacrifice of everything. The reference to the *via negativa* of the Spanish mystic St John of the Cross is followed by a repetition of the reassuring words of the English mystic Dame Julian of Norwich, and these, in turn, are fulfilled in a climactic image of reconciliation based on Dante's *Paradiso*. There the redeemed were gathered together in the form of a white rose. Here the pentecostal tongues of fire (the predominant image of this quartet) are enfolded in such a way as to resemble the petals of a rose so that fire and rose become the same image. The fire is the love of the Holy Spirit as well as the fire of purgation and the rose comes from the world of time, of natural beauty and love. The poem, therefore, ends with a vision of the union of the timeless with the temporal.

NOTES AND GLOSSARY:

an illegible stone: this refers back to the stones of 'East Coker' V: '. . . old stones that cannot be deciphered'

See, they return: the phrase is taken from a poem by Ezra Pound, 'The Return'

With the drawing ... Calling: Eliot is quoting from the second chapter of *The Cloud of Unknowing*, a fourteenth-century mystical treatise. Eliot considered that this work and the *Revelations of Divine Love* represented the two mystical extremes

Part 3

Commentary

Style

The fact that the Eliot of *Four Quartets* is a committed Christian has significant repercussions on the style of the poem. Eliot is a poet with a message and he would appear to have been influenced less by his recent experience of writing drama than by his recent exposure to Anglican pulpit oratory. The voice that addresses us in *Four Quartets* is often that of the preacher, conscious of the presence of a captive congregation, for instance, 'You say I am repeating / Something I have said before. I shall say it again'. The style is frequently rhetorical, as in 'Little Gidding' III, which is full of those syntactical repetitions and catalogues dear to the orator. For instance, the phrase 'I think of . . .' is repeated and followed by a list of the persons thus recalled, 'a king', 'three men, and more, on the scaffold', 'a few who died forgotten' and 'one who died blind and quiet'. The rhetorical question 'Why should we celebrate . . .' which succeeds provokes another spate of repetitions by way of response: 'It is not . . . Nor is it', 'We cannot' [twice], 'These men . . . and those . . . and those . . .', 'symbol' [twice]. Throughout the poem we find Eliot indulging in direct moral admonitions such as 'For us there is only the trying. The rest is not our business' or 'Old men ought to be explorers' or 'We must be still and still moving'. Sometimes Eliot's discourse is invested with biblical cadences as in 'East Coker' I where the style is based on that of Ecclesiastes. At the end of 'East Coker' III Eliot's voice becomes almost indistinguishable from that of another of his spiritual mentors, St John of the Cross.

An awareness of the primacy of spiritual values leads Eliot to be dismissive about the business of living. His search for 'that which is not world' results in the attainment of rare moments of ecstasy but it also leads to a preoccupation with negativity. Darkness is invoked to banish the images of everyday and the abstract diction often has a deliberately anti-sensual bias. Words such as 'deprivation', 'destitution', 'desiccation', 'abstention' are treated as positives in 'Burnt Norton' III, for instance. The anti-sensual impetus of Eliot's religion compelled him to seek an alternative to Shakespeare's densely metaphorical style. He turned to Dante as a model of stylistic asceticism, finding in the *Divine Comedy* 'the greatest austerity in the use of metaphor, simile, verbal beauty and elegance'. Although it is only in 'Little Gidding' that he attempts a conscious imitation of Dante's style, the staple verse of *Four Quartets* is stylistically austere. Much of the poetry is a poetry of statement, discursive rather than imagistic. There is a high proportion of abstract words and a paucity of adjectives, particularly in the third and fifth movements of each quartet, and, with the exception of 'Little Gidding', in the second part of the second movement as well. The lyrics (see following section The lyrics p.55) provide a welcome relief at regular intervals from the sermonising tone.

Most readers, however, would agree that the high points of the poem are those moments when Eliot modulates from discourse into a poetry of pure image. The alternation between discourse and image to a certain extent reflects the central antithesis of the poem which makes a qualitative distinction between the experience of everyday living and the intense perception of the visionary moment, the moment 'in and out of time'. Visionary moments are always rendered imagistically, the most notable instances being the rose-garden scene in 'Burnt Norton' I, the summer midnight scene in 'East Coker' I, and the description of midwinter spring in 'Little Gidding' I. The use of an imagistic technique is not, however, restricted to moments of ecstasy. The mention of the sea, in particular, seems to produce a sea-change in Eliot's style as, for instance, at the end of 'The Dry Salvages' I and II and 'East Coker' V. Such imagistic passages are often to be found embedded in a discursive context. Stylistically they are characterised by the use of concrete rather than abstract nouns, of particularising adjectives, of words indicative of time, place, weather and temperature.

Eliot considered 'the notion of appreciation of form without content' to be illusory. The discussion of particular passages in the detailed summaries (pp.13–51) shows how he uses his technical apparatus to underscore his meaning.

Structure and music

Walter Pater (1839–94), a forerunner of the Modernists, declared that 'All art aspires to the condition of music'. By calling his poem *Four Quartets*, Eliot is acknowledging the debt he owes to the art of music in finding a structure for the long poem. The idea of musical form had attracted him ever since he wrote 'Preludes' and 'Rhapsody on a Windy Night' at the beginning of his poetic career. Shortly before beginning work on the quartets he had written 'Five Finger Exercises' and two short poems under the title 'Words for Music', 'New Hampshire' and 'Virginia'. These later appeared in a collection of poems entitled 'Landscapes', a series of five poems in which images and themes are treated musically. Some of these images and themes reappear in *Four Quartets*. A quartet is more intricately organised structurally than either a prelude or a rhapsody. It has been suggested that Eliot had a specific string quartet in mind as he wrote and various works by Beethoven (1770–1827) and Bartók (1881–1945) have been put forward as models. Such theories are difficult to prove or disprove. Eliot's own view on musical form in poetry may be gleaned from his 1942 lecture 'The Music of Poetry', which provides a useful introduction to his method in *Four Quartets*. In this lecture he states that although he has not 'a technical knowledge of musical form' he believes that 'the properties in which music concerns the poet most nearly, are the sense of rhythm and the sense of structure'. On the matter of the relationship between poetic structure and musical structure he states:

> The use of recurrent themes is as natural to poetry as to music. There are possibilities for verse which bear some analogy to the development of a theme by different groups of instruments; there are possibilities of transitions in a poem comparable to the different movements of a symphony or a quartet; there are possibilities of contrapuntal arrangement of subject-matter.

As the title indicates, each of the four poems is structurally a poetic equivalent of a classical symphony, quartet or sonata. Their structure is far more rigid than one might realise from reading them as separate poems. Each of the quartets consists of five movements and each of these movements in turn has its own inner structure which recurs with slight variations in all four quartets. For instance, one obvious example is the way in which the second movement in each quartet begins with a lyric movement which is followed by an unrhymed passage in spoken idiom.

The analogy with musical form goes much deeper than a comparison of the five sections in each quartet with the movements of a musical quartet. In addition to its external similarity to musical form Eliot's poem is musical in its internal organisation. In *Some Aspects of the Novel* (1927) E.M. Forster (1879–1970) discusses the device of repeating a 'little phrase' as a subtle musical mode of organising literature. He points out that such a mode of organisation gives a work of art unity and homogeneity. It binds its disparate parts into a coherent whole. In *Four Quartets* images, phrases and words are played again and again with modifications within one quartet, and are also repeated from quartet to quartet. Recurring images are those of the dance, pattern and rhythm, darkness and light, ascent and descent, roses and yew, land, sea and river, journeying and, in particular, the London Underground. If we glance at the beginning and end of *Four Quartets*, for instance, we notice that the first section of 'Burnt Norton' contains the visit to the rose-garden while the concluding image in 'Little Gidding' is of the union of fire and rose. In between the rose has appeared in several other symbolic guises. 'Late roses filled with early snow' have served as an image of universal disruption in 'East Coker' II. In 'Dry Salvages' I a sense of the menace of the sea is evoked through the image, 'the salt is on the briar rose'. Later in 'Dry Salvages' IV we read of purgatorial fires of which 'the flame is roses and the smoke is briars', an image which anticipates the conclusion of the poem. An allusion to 'the Royal Rose' in 'Dry Salvages' III appears to be connected to 'the spectre of a Rose' in 'Little Gidding' III and to refer to the Wars of the Roses, an employment of the image for purposes of historical reference. The 'spectre of a Rose' also has other connotations (see p.48). A similar series of musical echoes is set up by means of literary allusions. Most of these have a certain homogeneity in that they are drawn from religious literature, from the Bible, the writings of Christian mystics or from Milton's *Samson Agonistes* and Dante's *Divine Comedy*. In addition, phrases from these works recur like a refrain, for instance 'in the middle way' or 'all shall be well'. A recurrent thematic preoccupation with time and the timeless is reflected in the high degree of repetition of words with temporal associations, for instance, 'present', 'past', 'future', 'before', 'after', 'now', 'always', 'never', 'moment', 'end' and 'beginning'. These words recur in isolation in a variety of combinations and permutations. The spatial equivalent of this concern with time and the timeless is reflected in Eliot's preoccupation with stillness and movement, with the apparent paradox of 'the still point of the turning world'.

The lyrics

In each of the quartets there are two lyrics. These, by virtue of their brevity and highly formalised patterns, stand apart from the main body of the poem. The first introduces the second movement in each quartet, the second constitutes the entire fourth movement. The lyrics are so positioned, therefore, that they alternate with more discursive and meditative passages in each quartet and in this way contribute to the overall design. Eliot was of the opinion that 'in a poem of any length there must be passages of greater and less intensity to give a rhythm of fluctuating emotion essential to the musical structure of the whole'. The principal function of the lyrics in *Four Quartets* is to provide such moments of relief, to serve as interludes in the philosophical meditation.

The highly patterned form of the lyrics is also relevant to Eliot's concern with the role of form and pattern in his meditations on art and design in *Four Quartets*. In 'Burnt Norton' V, for instance, he observes,

> Only by the form, the pattern,
> Can words or music reach
> The stillness . . .

Elsewhere, commenting on the vexed question of formal pattern and free verse, Eliot says that it is assumed that modern poetry has done away with such forms as the sonnet, the formal ode, the ballade, the villanelle, rondeau or sestina. He, on the contrary, believes that 'the tendency to return to set, and even elaborate, patterns is permanent'. The subject of the first lyric in 'Burnt Norton' justifies Eliot's return to traditional measured verse since what he is writing about are universal rhythms and harmonies. The use of the lyrical form is at its most self-conscious here with images of song and dance being evoked within the verse. The repetition of 'figured' picks up the suggestions of 'dance' and anticipates the word 'pattern' in the concluding lines. The rhyme-scheme also offers an instance of intricate design consisting as it does of five triplets, one rhyme from each triplet being echoed in the next. These rhymes are masculine and strongly accented. The rhythm of the lines is uniform, four stresses per line, to enact the idea of a common universal rhythm, and, since Eliot is treating of a cosmic reconciliation, he does not fragment his lyric by dividing it into stanzas.

The most controversial of these highly patterned lyrics is the first lyric in 'The Dry Salvages'. The form employed here is the sestina, which Eliot had referred to as one of the most elaborate poetic forms and one disdained by modern poets. The sestina, a poem of six stanzas each of which adheres to the same rhyme-scheme, demands consider-able ingenuity of the English poet since English poetry is poor in rhymes. Eliot's choice of the sestina would appear to be justified by its appro-priateness to his subject matter. The very nature of this type of lyric with its repetitiveness in movement and rhyming is suggestive of the monotony being described. Rhymes are feminine throughout since Eliot is writing in a falling measure in keeping with the pessimism of his attitude. The device of enjambement prolongs the already quite lengthy lines to create an effect of long-drawn out boredom. The only pro-gression in the poem is in the use of the word 'annunciation'. Its associa-tion with disaster and death is finally transcended in the concluding word of the poem where Annunciation is capitalised and refers to the announcement of Christ's birth. The conclusion, therefore, points to a new beginning, a way out of the humdrum monotony of living which was the theme of the rest of the lyric. As a final example of Eliot's choice of measured forms which suit the exigencies of his subject matter let us turn to the second lyric in 'Little Gidding'. The duality which is the theme of this lyric is enacted in its structure. It is composed of two stanzas, each of which ends with a couplet. The use of an alternating rhyme-scheme also enforces the sense of duality. Eliot wishes to achieve a balance rather than a resolution. The choice between two responses to suffering is left open to the reader.

Commenting on the nature of lyric, Eliot remarks that 'certain forms are more appropriate to some periods than to others' and that a form can become 'fixed to the idiom of the moment of its perfection' and therefore be 'possessed by the mental outlook of a past generation'. In 'East Coker' II he has recourse to a lyric precisely to reflect the mental outlook of an earlier generation of poets, dismissing it as 'a periphrastic study in a worn out poetical fashion'. He follows it by an unrhymed colloquial verse paragraph to illustrate modern verse-writing technique. In 'East Coker' IV, on the other hand, he carries out a daring experiment in the updating of a Metaphysical lyric. The entire lyric is couched in the form of a Metaphysical conceit, describing a spiritual malady in terms of physical illness. The reference to charts, wires, endowed hospitals and a ruined millionaire provide the conceit with a contemporary frame of reference. However, these modern terms are counteracted by a series of words such as 'question', 'distempered', 'prevent' and 'substantial' which are used with a meaning which the *Oxford English Dictionary* labels as archaic, obsolete or rare. The wit of Metaphysical poetry is imitated in the numerous paradoxes, for instance, 'wounded surgeon', 'dying nurse', 'frigid . . . fires'. The central conceit also generates a number of paradoxes such as 'to be restored, our sickness must grow worse', 'if we do well, we shall/Die' and 'if to be warmed, then I must freeze'. 'East Coker' IV is an attempt at an 'easy commerce of old and new' in form and diction, but most critics regard it as a failure.

The variety of the lyric forms employed in *Four Quartets* reveals something of Eliot's musical versatility. Those short, compact poems not only provide relief from the discursive and frequently complex poetry of the rest of *Four Quartets* but also differ from each other in form and style and so contribute their share to the richness of the poem's overall texture.

Part 4

Hints for study

How to improve your understanding

(a) First familiarise yourself with the poem by frequent readings. Concentrate on one quartet at a time in the beginning.

(b) Study the Notes and Commentary supplied here and see that you understand each allusion in the quartets.

(c) Eliot frequently alludes to past writings, in particular to the Bible and to Dante. It is suggested that you read Ecclesiastes 3, Luke 1, John 1, Acts 2, Dante's *Inferno*, Cantos I and XV and *Paradiso* Canto XXXIV.

(d) Make sure that you have fully understood what Eliot is saying in each quartet by making brief summaries of each section for yourself.

(e) Examine the style in each section, the syntax, the imagery, the kind of vocabulary used, the tone adopted by Eliot.

(f) Once you have familiarised yourself with a quartet, focus on the relationship between its constituent parts. Look out for repetitions and near repetitions of theme, image and phraseology and observe whether any change or progression has occurred.

(g) When you have studied each of the quartets as a separate unit focus on the ways in which they are interrelated, again noting repetitions and variations on themes, images and diction.

Quotations appropriate to particular topics

As an indication of how to go about (f) and (g) above, here are examples of repetition of theme, image and diction.

(a) A recurrent theme—the need for asceticism: see 'Burnt Norton' III, 'East Coker' II, III and conclusion of V, 'The Dry Salvages V, 'Little Gidding' IV and V.

(b) Recurrent imagery—images of movement:
  (i) Journeying: see 'Burnt Norton' I (exploration), III, 'East Coker' II, III and V (exploration), 'The Dry Salvages' II, III and IV, 'Little Gidding' I, II and V (also exploration).
  (ii) Ascent and descent: see Epigraph, 'Burnt Norton' II, III, IV and V, 'East Coker' II, 'The Dry Salvages' III, 'Little Gidding' IV.

(iii) Dance: see 'Burnt Norton' II and V, 'East Coker' I, II and III, 'Little Gidding' II and V.
(c) Recurrent words—movement and stillness
    (i) Movement: see 'Burnt Norton' I, II, III and V, 'East Coker' III and V, 'The Dry Salvages' II and V, 'Little Gidding' II.
    (ii) Stillness: 'see 'Burnt Norton' II, III, IV and V, 'East Coker' III and V, 'Little Gidding' V.

Answering questions on poetry

(a) Read the question carefully several times and make sure that you understand what kind of answer it requires.

(b) Plan your answer by determining what are to be the main points in your essay. List these in the order that seems appropriate and select quotations from the poem which support them.

(c) In the introductory paragraph of your answer discuss the question set and give some general indication of the line of approach you intend to pursue in the essay. Then write what you have to say on the subject clearly and directly. Divide your essay into paragraphs, making one point in each paragraph and developing your views on this fully before moving on. Bring your answer to some kind of conclusion by pointing out what you have discovered or proved in the course of the essay.

(d) Do not include information which is irrelevant to the question you are answering. For instance, it is a waste of time to provide a brief biography of the poet as an introduction to an essay. One or two biographical facts may occasionally be relevant but a whole biography is hardly ever called for.

A sample question and answer

Discuss Eliot's treatment of the Second World War in *Four Quartets*.

Introduction

This theme may be discussed only in relation to three of the quartets since 'Burnt Norton' had been completed in 1935, four years before the outbreak of the Second World War. In his note on the genesis of *Four Quartets* Eliot tells us that the writing of the last three quartets was a direct outcome of the war. After the completion of 'Burnt Norton' he had become absorbed in the problem of writing for the stage and he might have abandoned poetry altogether were it not that the war made him introspective and destroyed his interest in drama for a time. 'East Coker' was conceived during this introspective phase and once having written it he began to envisage a set of four quartets. In his poem 'A Note on War Poetry' Eliot points out that one problem for the poet is that war is a special situation, it is not life; another is that the individual's experience of it is usually too large or too small. War poetry, however, must not be 'the expression of collective emotion'. Like all poetry, war poetry occurs only when 'private experience at its greatest intensity' becomes 'universal'. We shall now examine the three wartime quartets to see how Eliot succeeds in transcending the merely topical nature of wartime experience in his poetry.

Main Points

1. Eliot's approach in these wartime quartets is never documentary. (a) His early allusions to war are oblique. Illustrate from 'East Coker' II and III. It is only in 'Little Gidding' that he draws on it for imagery and setting. You could develop this idea. Even here the imagery tends to conceal the topicality of Eliot's references. For instance, the bomber plane is described as a 'dove descending' so that the superimposed images of bird and Holy Ghost blot out the visual image of the plane and it plays a symbolic rather than a realistic role. The principal war image of fire is similarly universalised into Heraclitean fire, Hercules's funeral pyre, Dante's 'refining fire', pentecostal fire and so on. You could develop this idea further. (b) The extent to which the war impinged on Eliot's consciousness may be inferred from the way in which war imagery occurs out of context in the poem. When he looks back on his literary career in 'East Coker', for instance, he sees it as spanning the years of '*L'entre deux guerres*' and he describes his attempt to master his craft in military metaphor as a 'raid' with 'shabby equipment' and 'undisciplined squads of emotion'. He also writes of conquests, of a fight to renew what has been lost, and so on.

2. The subject of war is universalised by being viewed through the historical perspective which Eliot had advocated in 'Tradition and the Individual Talent'. Here deal with 'The Dry Salvages' III—Krishna to Arjuna on the field of battle and the reference to the Wars of the Roses. Also write about the connection of Little Gidding with the English Civil War. Discuss Eliot's comments on the Civil War in 'Little Gidding' III.

3. (a) The real universality of the poem is due to the fact that it regards the problem of war not as a unique situation or an isolated phenomenon but as a manifestation of the fundamental human problem of suffering, pain and death. You could develop this idea further. (b) The use of elemental imagery helps to convey the fundamental nature of the problem. This is particularly true of Eliot's use of water imagery in 'The Dry Salvages' where river and sea function as destructive forces. The elemental image of fire also represents universal forces of destruction in 'Little Gidding'. You could develop these ideas further. 'Little Gidding'

II, in particular, is a *danse macabre* which illustrates the universality of human suffering through the four elemental images of air, earth, water and fire.

4. Eliot's personal and positive response to war has a universal relevance. He approaches the problem of human suffering as a Christian, measuring the suffering of war against the spiritual good which may come of suffering. (a) He is convinced that suffering is visited on man by a benevolent Deity and that it has a purgatorial effect: 'here as hereafter the alternative to hell is purgatory'. Develop with reference to 'East Coker' IV and 'Little Gidding' IV. In the latter, war is seen as a divine visitation similar to Pentecost. (b) The purgatorial effect of war may lead the individual soul to a state of mystical union with God. The connection of war with the 'dark night of the soul' is the subject of 'East Coker' III. Develop this idea. (c) A sense of the futility of human suffering and loss is admitted in 'The Dry Salvages' II, 'Where is there an end of it, the soundless wailing . . .?', but this yields to a Christian attitude of acceptance with the prayer of the one Annunciation which was, 'Be it done unto me according to thy word'. Eliot's consolatory attitude to war at the conclusion of his long poem is based on the revelations of the Christian mystic Dame Julian of Norwich, 'All shall be well'.

Conclusion
Far from writing a realistic account of his individual experience of war Eliot maintains a distance between the mind which suffered and the artist who creates. The war is usually treated allusively rather than directly. It is offered as a representative human experience of suffering and death rather than a unique topical situation. Not everyone will agree with Eliot's optimistic Christian attitude that negative experience is a necessary prelude to positive good but fair-minded critics must acknowledge that this is a poem in which 'private experience at its greatest intensity' achieves universality.

Some further questions
(1) 'Burnt Norton' was originally conceived as a complete poem. How successfully has it been integrated into *Four Quartets*?
(2) Consider Eliot's presentation of old age in 'East Coker' and 'Little Gidding'.
(3) 'The Dry Salvages' has been described as Eliot's 'American quartet'. Is this an apt description?
(4) What is the function of the shrine at Little Gidding in the last quartet?
(5) Comment on the use of pentecostal imagery in 'Little Gidding'.

(6) In what ways does the final section of 'Little Gidding' serve as a fitting conclusion to *Four Quartets*?

(7) Write an essay on the function of elemental imagery in any one quartet. (For instance, water imagery in 'The Dry Salvages', or fire imagery in 'Little Gidding').

(8) Take any one quartet and comment on its structural organisation.

(9) Write a stylistic commentary on one section of any quartet.

(10) Comment on the contribution made by the lyrics to any two quartets.

(11) Consider the part played by the Second World War in the last three quartets.

(12) Should the quotations from Heraclitus serve as an epigraph to *Four Quartets* as a whole or to 'Burnt Norton' only?

(13) What does a reader lose by reading the quartets as individual poems?

(14) Comment on the appropriateness of the title *Four Quartets*

(15) Write an essay entitled, 'Time as a poetic theme in *Four Quartets*'.

(16) Consider the part played by dance imagery in *Four Quartets*.

(17) Discuss the role of place-names in *Four Quartets*.

(18) Discuss Eliot's use of allusion to Dante's *Divine Comedy* in *Four Quartets*.

(19) Consider the ways in which the writings of the Christian mystics are deployed in *Four Quartets*.

(20) Write an essay on Eliot's treatment of literature as a theme in *Four Quartets*.

(21) 'Four Quartets presents a too negative view of human life to justify its reputation as a major poem.' Discuss.

Part 5

Suggestions for further reading

The text

ELIOT, T.S.: *Collected Poems 1909–1962*, Faber and Faber, London 1963. *Four Quartets* is also published separately by Faber in paperback, tenth impression 1979.

Other works by T.S. Eliot

KERMODE, FRANK (ED.): *Selected Prose of T.S. Eliot*, Faber and Faber, London, 1975.

Particularly recommended are the following essays: 'Reflections on Vers Libre' (1917), 'Tradition and the Individual Talent' (1919), 'Dante' (1929), 'Religion and Literature' (1935), 'Yeats' (1940), 'The Music of Poetry' (1942).

Books on T.S. Eliot

BERGONZI, BERNARD: *T.S. Eliot*, Macmillan, New York, 1972. A concise and readable introduction to Eliot's life and works.

HOWARTH, HERBERT: *Notes on Some Figures Behind T.S. Eliot*, Chatto and Windus, London, 1965. A useful study of the poet's intellectual and literary background.

KENNER, HUGH: *The Invisible Poet: T.S. Eliot*, Methuen, London, 1960. A lively and informative critical study of the poetry.

MATTHIESSEN, F.O.: *The Achievement of T.S. Eliot*, Oxford University Press, London, 1958. An early, illuminating survey of the poetry.

MOODY, A.D.: *Thomas Stearns Eliot, Poet*, Cambridge University Press, Cambridge, 1979. A recent critical study, erudite and full of stimulating critical comments.

SMITH, GROVER: *T.S. Eliot's Poetry and Plays: A Study in Sources and Meaning*, The University of Chicago Press, Chicago, 1974. Dull, but thorough and usually accurate.

SPENDER, STEPHEN: *Eliot*, Collins/Fontana, London, 1975. A short, interesting account.

STEAD, C.K.: *The New Poetic*, Pelican Books, London, 1964. Includes a controversial argument about the relative literary merits of *The Waste Land* and *Four Quartets*.

Books on Four Quartets

BERGONZI, BERNARD (ED.): *Four Quartets*, Casebook Series, Macmillan, London, 1969. A collection of useful critical essays.

GARDNER, HELEN: *The Composition of Four Quartets*, Faber and Faber, London, 1978. Contains drafts of the poems and correspondence about proposed alterations. Allows us to see Eliot's mind moving towards the final text.

GARDNER, HELEN: *The Art of T.S. Eliot*, Faber and Faber, London, 1968. Essays on various aspects of the poem and on its place in Eliot's *oeuvre*. Particularly good on the music of *Four Quartets*.

The author of these notes

MAIRE A. QUINN was educated at the Queen's University of Belfast and became a lecturer in the Royal University of Malta in 1972. Since 1974 she has been a lecturer in the English Department at Trinity College, Dublin. She has published articles on modern English and Anglo-Irish poetry, as well as on the short story. She is at present engaged in work on the short stories of Elizabeth Bowen.